21

STUDY GUIDE

International Relations: How Effectively Did the United States Contain the Spread of Communism?

CIE

app
available

Published by Clever Lili Limited.

contact@cleverlili.com

First published 2020

ISBN 978-1-913887-20-9

Cover by: Aquir on Adobe Stock

Icons by: flaticon and freepik

Contributors: Lynn Harkin, Nicola Nicholls, Megan Quirk, Jen Mellors

Edited by Paul Connolly and Rebecca Parsley

Design by Evgeni Veskov and Will Fox

DISCOVER MORE OF OUR IGCSE HISTORY STUDY GUIDES

GCSEHistory.com and Clever Lili

CIE

STUDY GUIDE

**International Relations:
Were the Peace Treaties of 1919-23 Fair?**

GCSEHistory.com

17

CIE

STUDY GUIDE

**International Relations:
To What Extent Was the League of
Nations a Success?**

GCSEHistory.com

18

CIE

STUDY GUIDE

**International Relations:
Why Had International Peace Collapsed
by 1939?**

GCSEHistory.com

19

CIE

STUDY GUIDE

**International Relations:
Who Was to Blame for the Cold War?**

GCSEHistory.com

20

CIE

STUDY GUIDE

**International Relations:
How Secure Was the USSR's Control Over
Eastern Europe, 1948 - 1989?**

GCSEHistory.com

22

CIE

STUDY GUIDE

**International Relations:
Why Did Events in the Gulf Matter
c1970 - 2000?**

GCSEHistory.com

23

CIE

STUDY GUIDE

The United States, 1919 - 1941

GCSEHistory.com

32

CIE

STUDY GUIDE

The First World War, 1914 - 1918

GCSEHistory.com

31

CIE

STUDY GUIDE

Russia, 1905 - 1941

GCSEHistory.com

33

CIE

STUDY GUIDE

Germany, 1918 - 1945

GCSEHistory.com

34

CIE

STUDY GUIDE

China, c1930-1990

GCSEHistory.com

46

THE GUIDES ARE EVEN BETTER WITH OUR GCSE/IGCSE HISTORY WEBSITE APP AND MOBILE APP

GCSE History is a text and voice web and mobile app that allows you to easily revise for your GCSE/IGCSE exams wherever you are - it's like having your own personal GCSE history tutor. Whether you're at home or on the bus, GCSE History provides you with thousands of convenient bite-sized facts to help you pass your exams with flying colours. We cover all topics - with more than 120,000 questions - across the Edexcel, AQA and CIE exam boards.

GCSEHistory.com

GET IT ON
Google Play

Download on the
App Store

Contents

In this study guide, you will see a series of icons, highlighted words and page references. The key below will help you quickly establish what these mean and where to go for more information.

Icons

WHAT questions cover the key events and themes.

WHO questions cover the key people involved.

WHEN questions cover the timings of key events.

WHERE questions cover the locations of key moments.

WHY questions cover the reasons behind key events.

HOW questions take a closer look at the way in which events, situations and trends occur.

IMPORTANCE questions take a closer look at the significance of events, situations, and recurrent trends and themes.

DECISIONS questions take a closer look at choices made at events and situations during this era.

Highlighted words

Abdicate - occasionally, you will see certain words highlighted within an answer. This means that, if you need it, you'll find an explanation of the word or phrase in the glossary which starts on **page 72**.

Page references

Tudor *(p. 7)* - occasionally, a certain subject within an answer is covered in more depth on a different page. If you'd like to learn more about it, you can go directly to the page indicated.

The title of the fifth unit in the Core Content of Option B in the CiE History iGCSE is 'How effectively did the USA contain the spread of communism?' This unit investigates the American containment policies of the 1950s -1970s.

Purpose
This unit focuses on international relations and the way in which different nation states interacted, and the change, continuity and significance of their relationships over time. You will study their priorities, agreements, disagreements and the key events that affected them.

Enquiries
This unit gives you the information you need to understand the following:

- The United States and events in Korea, 1950 - 53.
- The United States and events in Cuba, 1959 - 62.
- American involvement in Vietnam.

Topics
Topics covered in this course include:

- American reactions to North Korea's invasion of South Korea, the involvement of the UN and the course of the war to 1953.
- American reactions to the Cuban revolution, including the missiles crisis and its aftermath.
- American involvement in Vietnam, the reasons for it, tactics and strategy, and the reasons for the withdrawal.

Key Individuals
Key individuals studied in this course include:

- Kim Il-sung.
- Harry S Truman.
- General MacArthur.
- Dwight Eisenhower.
- Fidel Castro.
- John F Kennedy.
- Ho Chi Minh.
- Ngo Dinh Diem.
- Lyndon B Johnson.
- Richard Nixon.

Assessment
This unit usually appears as one of four possible questions in Option B Core Content International Relations Since 1919 on the Paper 1 exam, of which you must complete two. Therefore, you will answer one question on the success of the League of Nations, if this appears as an option on your exam paper. The question is comprised of 3 sections; a), b), and c). However, check with your teacher to find out whether this unit will appear on the Paper 2 source paper in your exam.

- On the Paper 1 exam, you may choose to complete a three-part question on this topic, which will be divided into sections a), b) and c).

- Question a is worth 4 marks. This question will require you to describe key features of the time period. You will be asked to recall 2 relevant points and support them with details or provide at least four relevant points without supporting detail.

- Question b is worth 6 marks. This question will require you to explain a key event or development. You will need to identify two reasons, support those reasons with relevant factual detail and then explain how the reasons made the event occur.

- Question c is worth 10 marks. This question will require you to construct an argument to support and challenge an interpretation stated in the question. You will need to have a minimum of three explanations in total and fully evaluate to come to a justified conclusion. The best approach is to discuss two arguments on one side of the debate, and two arguments on the other, before coming to a brief conclusion. You will have the opportunity to show your ability to explain and analyse historical events using 2nd order concepts such as causation, consequence, change, continuity, similarity and difference.

If this topic appears on Paper 2, you will answer six questions on a range of source material about this topic. Check with your teacher to find out your Paper 2 topic.

If this topic appears on Paper 2, you will answer six questions on a range of source material about this topic. Check with your teacher to find out your Paper 2 topic.

Revision! A dreaded word. Everyone knows it's coming, everyone knows how much it helps with your exam performance, and everyone struggles to get started! We know you want to do the best you can in your IGCSEs, but schools aren't always clear on the best way to revise. This can leave students wondering:

✔ How should I plan my revision time?

✔ How can I beat procrastination?

✔ What methods should I use? Flash cards? Re-reading my notes? Highlighting?

Luckily, you no longer need to guess at the answers. Education researchers have looked at all the available revision studies, and the jury is in. They've come up with some key pointers on the best ways to revise, as well as some thoughts on popular revision methods that aren't so helpful. The next few pages will help you understand what we know about the best revision methods.

How can I beat procrastination?

This is an age-old question, and it applies to adults as well! Have a look at our top three tips below.

Reward yourself

When we think a task we have to do is going to be boring, hard or uncomfortable, we often put if off and do something more 'fun' instead. But we often don't really enjoy the 'fun' activity because we feel guilty about avoiding what we should be doing. Instead, get your work done and promise yourself a reward after you complete it. Whatever treat you choose will seem all the sweeter, and you'll feel proud for doing something you found difficult. Just do it!

Just do it!

We tend to procrastinate when we think the task we have to do is going to be difficult or dull. The funny thing is, the most uncomfortable part is usually making ourselves sit down and start it in the first place. Once you begin, it's usually not nearly as bad as you anticipated.

Pomodoro technique

The pomodoro technique helps you trick your brain by telling it you only have to focus for a short time. Set a timer for 20 minutes and focus that whole period on your revision. Turn off your phone, clear your desk, and work. At the end of the 20 minutes, you get to take a break for five. Then, do another 20 minutes. You'll usually find your rhythm and it becomes easier to carry on because it's only for a short, defined chunk of time.

Spaced practice

We tend to arrange our revision into big blocks. For example, you might tell yourself: "This week I'll do all my revision for the Cold War, then next week I'll do the Medicine Through Time unit."

This is called **massed practice**, because all revision for a single topic is done as one big mass.

But there's a better way! Try **spaced practice** instead. Instead of putting all revision sessions for one topic into a single block, space them out. See the example below for how it works.

This means planning ahead, rather than leaving revision to the last minute - but the evidence strongly suggests it's worth it. You'll remember much more from your revision if you use **spaced practice** rather than organising it into big blocks. Whichever method you choose, though, remember to reward yourself with breaks.

Spaced practice (more effective):

week 1	week 2	week 3	week 4
Topic 1	Topic 1	Topic 1	Topic 1
Topic 2	Topic 2	Topic 2	Topic 2
Topic 3	Topic 3	Topic 3	Topic 3
Topic 4	Topic 4	Topic 4	Topic 4

Massed practice (less effective)

week 1	week 2	week 3	week 4
Topic 1	Topic 2	Topic 3	Topic 4

What methods should I use to revise?

Self-testing/flash cards

Self explanation/mind-mapping

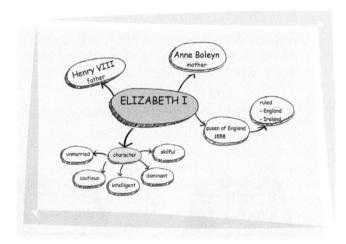

The research shows a clear winner for revision methods - **self-testing**. A good way to do this is with **flash cards.** Flash cards are really useful for helping you recall short – but important – pieces of information, like names and dates.

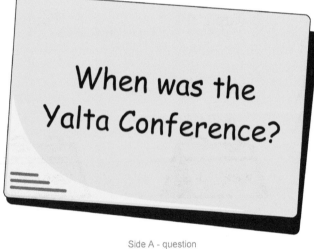

Side A - question

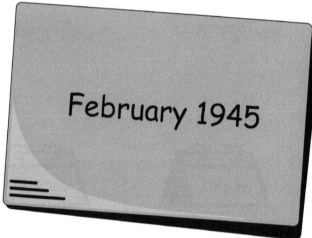

Side B - answer

Write questions on one side of the cards, and the answers on the back. This makes answering the questions and then testing yourself easy. Put all the cards you get right in a pile to one side, and only repeat the test with the ones you got wrong - this will force you to work on your weaker areas.

pile with right answers

pile with wrong answers

As this book has a quiz question structure itself, you can use it for this technique.

Another good revision method is **self-explanation**. This is where you explain how and why one piece of information from your course linked with another piece.

This can be done with **mind-maps,** where you draw the links and then write explanations for how they connect. For example, President Truman is connected with anti-communism because of the Truman Doctrine.

Quizzes, amazing exam preparation tools and more at GCSEHistory.com

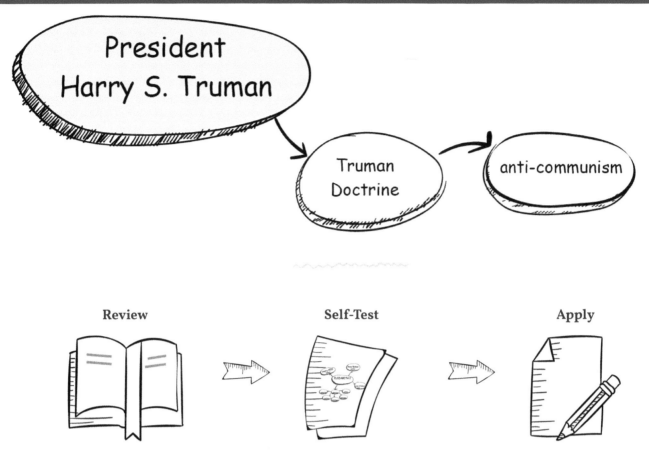

Review

Self-Test

Apply

Start by highlighting or re-reading to create your flashcards for self-testing.

Test yourself with flash cards. Make mind maps to explain the concepts.

Apply your knowledge on practice exam questions.

 Which revision techniques should I be cautious about?

Highlighting and **re-reading** are not necessarily bad strategies - but the research does say they're less effective than flash cards and mind-maps.

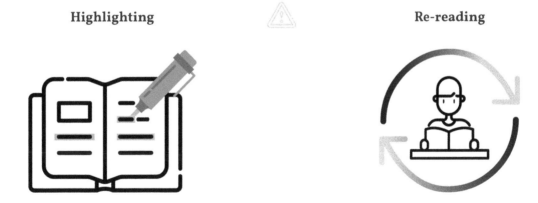

Highlighting

Re-reading

If you do use these methods, make sure they are **the first step to creating flash cards**. Really engage with the material as you go, rather than switching to autopilot.

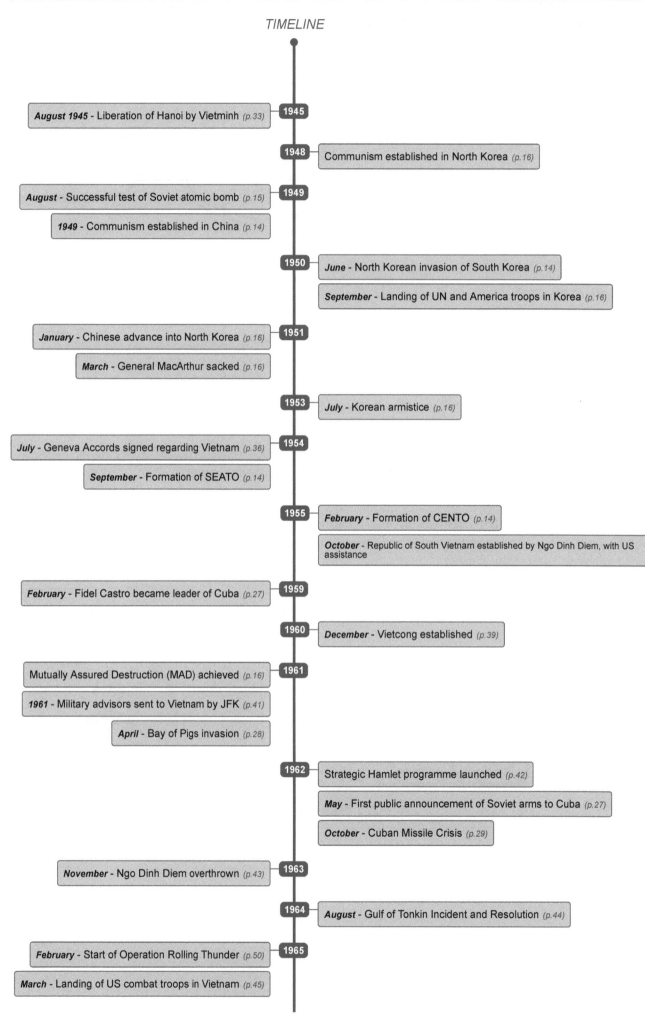

TIMELINE

August 1945 - Liberation of Hanoi by Vietminh *(p.33)* — **1945**

1948 — Communism established in North Korea *(p.16)*

August - Successful test of Soviet atomic bomb *(p.15)* — **1949**

1949 - Communism established in China *(p.14)*

1950 — **June** - North Korean invasion of South Korea *(p.14)*

September - Landing of UN and America troops in Korea *(p.16)*

January - Chinese advance into North Korea *(p.16)* — **1951**

March - General MacArthur sacked *(p.16)*

1953 — **July** - Korean armistice *(p.16)*

July - Geneva Accords signed regarding Vietnam *(p.36)* — **1954**

September - Formation of SEATO *(p.14)*

1955 — **February** - Formation of CENTO *(p.14)*

October - Republic of South Vietnam established by Ngo Dinh Diem, with US assistance

February - Fidel Castro became leader of Cuba *(p.27)* — **1959**

1960 — **December** - Vietcong established *(p.39)*

Mutually Assured Destruction (MAD) achieved *(p.16)* — **1961**

1961 - Military advisors sent to Vietnam by JFK *(p.41)*

April - Bay of Pigs invasion *(p.28)*

1962 — Strategic Hamlet programme launched *(p.42)*

May - First public announcement of Soviet arms to Cuba *(p.27)*

October - Cuban Missile Crisis *(p.29)*

November - Ngo Dinh Diem overthrown *(p.43)* — **1963**

1964 — **August** - Gulf of Tonkin Incident and Resolution *(p.44)*

February - Start of Operation Rolling Thunder *(p.50)* — **1965**

March - Landing of US combat troops in Vietnam *(p.45)*

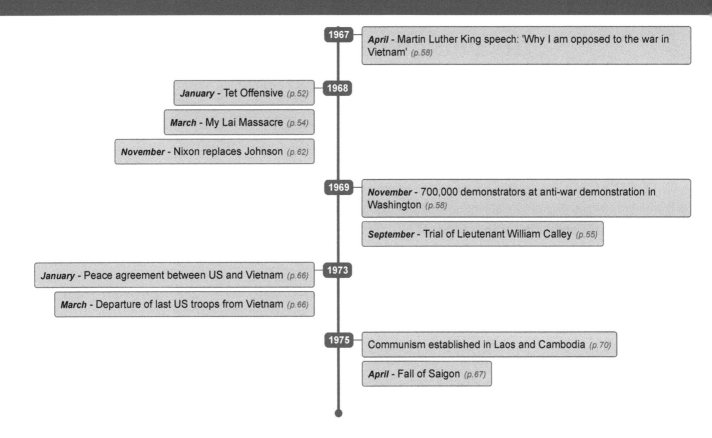

1967

April - Martin Luther King speech: 'Why I am opposed to the war in Vietnam' *(p.58)*

1968

January - Tet Offensive *(p.52)*

March - My Lai Massacre *(p.54)*

November - Nixon replaces Johnson *(p.62)*

1969

November - 700,000 demonstrators at anti-war demonstration in Washington *(p.58)*

September - Trial of Lieutenant William Calley *(p.55)*

1973

January - Peace agreement between US and Vietnam *(p.66)*

March - Departure of last US troops from Vietnam *(p.66)*

1975

Communism established in Laos and Cambodia *(p.70)*

April - Fall of Saigon *(p.67)*

THE PRINCIPLE OF CONTAINMENT

'The main element of any United States policy toward the Soviet Union must be that of a long-term, patient but firm and vigilant containment...'
George Kennan, 1947

 What was containment?

Containment *(p.70)* was America's policy on communism. It involved preventing it from spreading to new countries, rather than attacking existing communist nations.

 When was containment introduced?

Containment *(p.70)* was first introduced in 1947.

 What policy introduced the idea of containment?

Containment *(p.70)* was first set out in the Truman Doctrine and the Marshall Plan.

 What methods of containment were used?

The USA used 4 main methods of containment *(p.70)*:

- ☑ It aimed to build bigger and better weapons faster than the USSR. This led to both sides becoming embroiled in an arms race.
- ☑ It offered economic support for countries threatened by communism.
- ☑ It forged alliances with other countries.
- ☑ It gave military assistance to countries threatened by communism.

 Why was containment needed?

After the Second World War, the apparent need for containment *(p.70)* was reinforced by 4 main global events:

- ☑ In 1947-48, eastern European countries were taken over by communist governments.
- ☑ In 1948, North Korea became communist.
- ☑ In August 1949, the USSR successfully tested an atomic bomb.
- ☑ China became a communist country in 1949.

 What alliances were formed as part of containment?

The USA formed 4 main alliances in response to the threat of communism:

- ☑ The most important was the North Atlantic Treaty Organisation, or NATO, formed in 1949.
- ☑ The South-East Asia Treaty Organisation (SEATO) was formed in September 1954 between the USA, New Zealand, Australia, the Philippines, Thailand, Pakistan, Britain and France.
- ☑ CENTO, or the Central Treaty Organisation, was formed in February 1955 between Iran, Iraq, Pakistan, Turkey and the UK.
- ☑ The USSR responded by setting up the Warsaw Pact in May 1955. The USSR, Romania, Bulgaria, Czechoslovakia, East Germany, Albania, Poland and Hungary were members.

 How was military assistance used as part of containment?

The USA was prepared to provide weapons, military advice, training, troops, technical support and personnel to countries threatened by communism.

When was military assistance used as part of containment?

Examples of 3 significant occasions when the USA provided military support for countries threatened by communism were:

- ☑ 1950 - 1953 - in Korea, with UN support.
- ☑ 1961 - The Bay of Pigs invasion in Cuba.
- ☑ 1955 - 1975 - Vietnam.

DID YOU KNOW?

George Kennan, the author of the 'Long Telegram', later published his original ideas about containment under the pseudonym 'Mr X'.

THE ARMS RACE

'If you go on with this nuclear arms race, all you are going to do is make the rubble bounce'.
Winston Churchill, 1949

What was the arms race?

The arms race was a competition between the USA and the USSR to gain military dominance by developing their nuclear capabilities and weapons.

 ### When was the arms race?

The Soviet Union emerged as a nuclear power in 1949, leading to the arms race with the USA. This lasted until the end of the Cold War in 1990.

 ### What was the importance of the arms race?

The arms race was important for 2 main reasons:

- ☑ It led to the fear of mutually assured destruction as both sides had enough weapons to destroy the world many times over.
- ☑ The USA and the USSR had to find ways to solve disputes that did not result in a nuclear war.

 ### What were the most important events of the arms race?

There were 6 main military achievements and events during the arms race:

- ☑ 1945 - the USA dropped atomic bombs on Hiroshima and Nagasaki, bringing the Second World War to an end.
- ☑ 1949 - the USSR tested an atomic bomb.
- ☑ 1952 - the USA developed the hydrogen bomb.
- ☑ 1953 - the USSR tested its own hydrogen bomb.
- ☑ 1957 - both the USA and USSR successfully tested intercontinental ballistic missiles (ICBMs).
- ☑ 1962 - the Cuban Missile Crisis *(p.29)* was the highest point of tension in the arms race.

 ### What role did brinkmanship play in the arms race?

Brinkmanship was important in the arms race because:

- ☑ An enemy could be forced to back down in a moment of crisis by pushing it to the brink of an unwanted war.

☑ To make any threats credible, both sides needed nuclear weapons.

☑ The Cuban Missile Crisis *(p.29)* is an example of brinkmanship. The USA and the USSR were very close to a nuclear war, with both sides threatening conflict until the USSR backed down.

 What was the theory of mutually assured destruction, or MAD in the arms race?

Mutually assured destruction, or MAD, was the following theory:

☑ It had developed by the 1960s.

☑ It stated that if either the USA or the USSR used their nuclear weapons, both would be destroyed. Each possessed so many, the damage would be unimaginable.

☑ It was believed war would be prevented because both sides feared it; a nuclear war was, in theory, unwinnable.

 What was nuclear utilisation target selection in the arms race?

Nuclear utilisation target selection theory, or NUTs:

☑ Developed in the 1980s.

☑ Was a theory President Reagan believed in. He thought a limited nuclear war was possible as long as the USA struck at the USSR first and wiped out its nuclear weapons.

 What were intercontinental ballistic missiles in the arms race?

Intercontinental ballistic missiles, called ICBMs, were nuclear-armed ballistic missiles with a range of more than 3,500 miles.

 What were anti-ballistic missiles in the arms race?

Anti-ballistic missiles were missiles that would intercept and destroy other ballistic missiles. The USA and the USSR developed ABMs in the 1960s.

 What were multiple independent reentry vehicles in the arms race?

Multiple independent reentry vehicles (MIRVs) were developed in 1968. These missiles carried multiple warheads which could each be independently targeted.

DID YOU KNOW?

In October 1961, the USSR tested their largest nuclear weapon, the Tsar Bomba, creating the most powerful man-made explosion ever seen.

The explosion yielded 58 megatons of TNT, and the blast waves from the test were recorded as travelling three times around the earth.

THE KOREAN WAR, 1950 - 1953

'If we let Korea down, the Soviet[s] will keep right on going and swallow up one [place] after another.'
President Harry Truman, 1950

 What was the Korean War?

The Korean War was fought between North and South Korea and was the first flashpoint of the Cold War in Asia.

Where did the Korean War take place?

In Korea, which is between China to the west and Japan to the east.

 When was the Korean War?

The Korean War began in June 1950 and finished in 1954.

 What were the key phases of the Korean War?

There were 5 main phases to the war, including:

- [x] North Korea invaded South Korea on 25th June, 1950.
- [x] A UN army, made up mostly of American military and led by General Douglas MacArthur, arrived in Korea in September 1950 to push back against the North Korean invasion *(p.20)*.
- [x] In October 1950, UN forces advanced into North Korean territory.
- [x] On 25th October, China entered the war. Together with the North Korean army, they pushed the UN forces back below the 38th parallel. This resulted in a stalemate for over two years.
- [x] After peace talks on 27th July, 1953, the UN, China and North Korea signed a peace treaty.

 What were the long-term causes that led to the Korean War?

Several important long-term events led to the Korean War, including:

- [x] The history of Korea was shaped by many wars over who would control it. Both China and Japan ruled the nation for significant periods of time.
- [x] Between 1910 and 1945, Korea was controlled by Japan. This changed at the end of the Second World War.
- [x] At the end of the Second World War, the Japanese in the north surrendered to the USSR, and those in the south to the USA.

 At the end of the Second World War, what was the situation that led to the Korean War?

At the end of the Second World War, when Japan surrendered and Korea was occupied by Soviet troops in the north and American troops in the south, the following happened:

- [x] The country was divided into two separate zones along the 38th parallel, a circle of latitude that runs across the middle of Korea.
- [x] The division of Korea was supposed to be temporary. The aim was for it to be a united and independent country. The United Nations was to organise elections that would achieve this.
- [x] Instead of free elections, the Soviets in North Korea enabled Korean communist Kim Il-Sung to take control of the nation without being elected.
- [x] There was an election in US-controlled South Korea, and USA supporter and capitalist figure Syngman Rhee became its leader.
- [x] At this point, North and South Korea became two different nations. The USSR zone in the north became the People's Republic of Korea, and the US zone in the south became the Republic of Korea.
- [x] While the leaders in both North and South Korea were nationalists and wanted a united country after the war, they wanted the nation to be led by different ideologies - capitalism in the south and communism in the north.

 Who ran North Korea at the time of the Korean War?

After 1947, the government in North Korea was the communist Democratic People's Republic led by Kim Il-Sung. The capital was Pyongyang.

 Who ran South Korea at the time of the Korean War?

After 1947, the government in South Korea was the non-communist Republic of Korea led by Syngman Rhee. Its capital was Seoul.

What were the key events in the build-up to the Korean War?

The leaders of North and South Korea each saw themselves as the legitimate and rightful ruler of the whole nation. Events in the build-up to the Korean War included:

- ☑ Due to the attitude of superiority from both sides there were a number of clashes on the border between North and South Korea.

- ☑ Kim Il-Sung, the leader of North Korea, visited Stalin in 1949 to ask for his support in an invasion of South Korea. He felt this would be welcome in the south as an effort to reunite the two nations.

- ☑ Stalin did not think it was the right time as he did not want a fight against US troops still stationed in South Korea.

- ☑ In 1950, Stalin's circumstances had changed. The US troops had left South Korea; communists were in power in China; and the USSR had its own nuclear weapons and had cracked the secret codes used by the USA to talk to other nations. As a result, Stalin felt any future actions in Korea would not meet American opposition.

- ☑ Stalin began sending tanks, artillery and aircraft to North Korea and gave the go-ahead for an invasion of the south.

- ☑ Stalin stated USSR soldiers would not be directly involved, and if further supplies were needed North Korea should ask China.

 What started the Korean War?

The Korean War broke out when North Korea invaded South Korea on 25th June, 1950.

 Why did the UN get involved in the Korean War?

When the south was invaded, the USA brought the matter to the UN which passed a resolution calling for North Korea to withdraw. When it did not, the UN sent international troops - mostly American - to force it out. In this way the USA could argue it was acting against international aggression rather than following its containment policy *(p.14)*.

 Why did America get involved in the Korean War?

There were 3 key reasons America got involved in the Korean War:

- ☑ President Truman was concerned communism was spreading in Asia.

- ☑ China's fall to communism in 1949 heightened this fear.

- ☑ Truman was also concerned about Stalin's use of Cominform to encourage countries to turn to communism.

 What was America's role in the Korean War?

America had 2 main roles in the Korean War:

- ☑ United Nations troops, mainly American and led by US General Douglas MacArthur, were sent to Korea. The North was supported by the Soviet Union.

- ☑ UN forces were able to push North Korea back to the Chinese border, but in late 1950 China joined the war and the UN had to retreat.

 What ended the Korean War?

After three years of fighting an armistice was agreed, which re-established the border between North and South Korea.

 What effect did the Korean War have on America?

There were 5 main consequences of the Korean War:

- ☑ It demonstrated the USA's commitment to containing communism and led to a tripling of military spending to prevent its spread.

- ☑ To stop the spread of communism in Asia, the Southeast Asia Treaty Organisation (SEATO) was set up in September 1954. Britain, Pakistan, USA, Thailand, France, Australia, the Philippines and New Zealand all joined.

- ☑ The sacking of General MacArthur over his proposal to deploy nuclear bombs against North Korea underlined the USA's caution with regard to using nuclear weapons.

✅ The Soviet Union doubled the size of the Red Army, from 2.8 million in 1950 to 5.6 million in 1955.

✅ As the war did not escalate further, it showed neither superpower was prepared to engage in direct military confrontation with the other, preferring instead to fight proxy wars.

 ## What happened in the Korean War?

The fighting in Korea took place in mountains, ravines and swamps - terrain that was more familiar to the Koreans and Chinese than the UN. They also had to contend with terrible cold and snowstorms in winter.

 ## What were the main events of the Korean War?

The Korean War progressed in a number of stages:

✅ Between September and October 1950, the UN was successful in pushing North Korean troops back out of South Korea.

✅ Between October and November 1950, the UN troops crossed over the 38th parallel and pushed the North Korean troops north in an attempt to defeat the communists and reunite the country.

✅ Between November 1950 and January 1951, Chinese forces launched a counteroffensive and pushed the UN troops back past the 38th parallel.

✅ The UN counter-attacked between January and July 1951 and retook Seoul.

✅ The war then settled into a stalemate which lasted for two years, from July 1951 to July 1953.

 ## How successful was the UN in Korean War?

In the initial stages of their involvement, UN troops were successful in pushing back the North Korean troops.

✅ Some UN troops joined the South Korean forces in Pusan and pushed past the Pusan perimeter.

✅ Others, led by General MacArthur, invaded behind the communist lines at Inchon.

✅ Seoul was liberated from the communists and North Korean troops were pushed back to the 38th parallel.

 ## Why did the UN invade North Korea during the Korean War ?

From October 1950, after UN troops had liberated South Korea, they began to invade North Korea.

✅ The UN troops crossed the 38th parallel in an attempt to achieve the UN objective of a 'unified, independent and democratic government' for all of Korea.

✅ Pyongyang was captured on 19th October.

✅ By November, some American forces had reached the Yalu River on the border with China.

 ## How did China get involved in the Korean War?

There were 4 key events:

✅ As UN troops approached its borders, China feared an invasion of its territory and launched a huge counter-attack of 200,000 soldiers.

✅ UN forces were driven south, back over the 38th parallel.

✅ Seoul was recaptured by communist forces.

✅ The UN forces eventually stabilised around the 37th parallel.

 ## How did the UN react to the Chinese invasion of Korea during the Korean War?

In January 1951 the UN counter-attacked the Chinese and North Korean forces, pushing them back to the 38th parallel and retaking Seoul.

What was the stalemate in the Korean War?

Between July 1951 and July 1953, while negotiations were ongoing, fighting continued along a fortified frontier near the 39th parallel. This cost many lives but gained little territory.

 Why was the Armistice signed in the Korean War?

In July 1953 an armistice was signed that agreed a border very similar to that of the 38th parallel. This was for a number of reasons.

- ☑ Eisenhower had replaced Truman as president and was keen to end the war.
- ☑ Stalin's death in 1953 made China and North Korea less confident.

 How many people were killed in the Korean War?

There were a number of costs to the Korean War:

- ☑ 30,000 American troops were killed.
- ☑ 4,500 UN troops from other countries were killed.
- ☑ Approximately 70,000 South Korean soldiers died.
- ☑ About 500,000 South Korean civilians were killed.
- ☑ An estimated 780,000 North Korean and Chinese soldiers and civilians died in the war.

 What was the fighting like in the Korean War?

The fighting in Korea took place in mountains, ravines and swamps - terrain that was more familiar to the Koreans and Chinese than the UN. They also had to contend with terrible cold and snowstorms in winter.

DID YOU KNOW?

The 38th parallel had been suggested before as a way of dividing Korea.

Japan suggested to Russia that they split Korea along the 38th parallel in 1896.

THE INVASION OF SOUTH KOREA, JUNE 1950

'War is not only a contest of strength, but also a test of morality and ethics'.
Kim Il-Sung,

 What happened when North Korea invaded South Korea?

The Korean War *(p. 16)* broke out when North Korea invaded South Korea and sent troops over the 38th parallel.

 When did North Korea invade South Korea?

North Korea invaded South Korea on 25th June, 1950.

 Why did North Korea invade South Korea?

North Korea invaded South Korea for 5 key reasons:

- ☑ North Korea invaded the south because Kim Il-Sung wanted to unite Korea under communist rule. By June 1950, he was confident an invasion would be successful.

- ✅ Kim Il-Sung had the support of communist leaders - Stalin in the USSR, and Mao Zedong in China.
- ✅ North Korea's armed forces were stronger than those of South Korea. The USSR had provided tanks, planes and heavy artillery.
- ✅ China became communist in 1949 and, after August that year, the USSR had the atom bomb. Kim Il-Sung thought these factors would deter a US response.
- ✅ American politicians had made speeches suggesting Korea was not seen as a priority.

Why were North Korean troops able to invade South Korea so easily?

Very few American troops were available to help the South Koreans defend their territory, making it easier for the north to invade.

What was the significance of North Korea's invasion of South Korea?

North Korea's invasion of South Korea was significant because it triggered a large-scale conflict that would last for 3 years and become the first hotspot of the Cold War in Asia.

DID YOU KNOW?

The Korean War is the name given to the conflict by the west.

In North Korea, it is known as the Fatherland Liberation War, while in South Korea it is called Six-Two-Five because it began on the 25th June.

RETALIATION BY THE UN

'If the UN cannot bring the crisis in Korea to an end then we might as well just wash up the United Nations and forget it'.
US Senator Tom Connally

❓ What was the response of the United Nations to the invasion of South Korea by North Korea?

When North Korea invaded South Korea, the Security Council of the United Nations met on the same day - 25th June, 1950.

What was the UN's decision about South Korea following the invasion?

In the days following the invasion of South Korea, the UN passed 3 resolutions on the matter:

- ✅ The first, on 25th June, called the invasion a 'breach of the peace' and called for North Korea to withdraw its troops.
- ✅ The second, on 27th June, recommended that member nations of the UN should supply troops to stop the invasion.
- ✅ The third, on 7th July, recommended the UN troops come under the command of the USA.

How did North Korea react to the United Nation's resolutions in response to the invasion of South Korea?

North Korea ignored the UN's first resolution, that ordered them to withdraw its troops.

Why did the UN support South Korea after they were invaded in 1950?

The UN was able to pass resolutions condemning North Korea because the USSR was not present. The Soviets were boycotting the UN because of the organisation's refusal to admit communist China as a member.

Which countries supplied troops for the UN in South Korea after the invasion?

Troops from the USA and 15 other countries, including Britain and France, were sent to assist South Korea. The USA supplied the majority of the support given.

 Why was MacArthur dismissed as the leader of the UN forces after the invasion of South Korea?

MacArthur and Truman disagreed about how to fight the war. Truman wanted a more discreet approach to avoid an all out war in Asia but MacArthur wanted to bomb China and even suggested using nuclear weapons to end the war. As a result, MacArthur was removed.

DID YOU KNOW?

North and South Korea were admitted into the UN in 1991.

AMERICAN INVOLVEMENT IN KOREA

'It is fatal to enter an war without the will to win it.'
General Douglas MacArthur

 What was America's response to the invasion of South Korea?

The USA put pressure on the United Nations to condemn the North Korean invasion *(p.20)*. It took control of the subsequent UN invasion and supplied by far the largest number of troops.

 Why did America defend South Korea during the invasion?

America had a number of reasons for wanting to defend South Korea, and for pressuring the UN to become involved:

- ☑ It had been involved in establishing the Republic of Korea.
- ☑ It was determined, under its policy of containment *(p.70)*, to prevent further communist expansion.
- ☑ It was concerned the invasion of South Korea might encourage a Chinese attack on Formosa (Taiwan) and lead to a massive shift in world power from capitalism to communism.
- ☑ If the UN had failed to act, it is likely America would have taken action on its own to prevent this.
- ☑ Truman wanted to avoid the mistakes of the 1930s. There would be no appeasement and the USA would support the UN to ensure it did not fail as the League of Nations had.

 How was the UN influenced by America in the invasion of South Korea?

The United Nations' action in Korea was very much influenced by the USA.

- ☑ The UN forces were commanded by General MacArthur, an American.
- ☑ Half the ground forces were American.
- ☑ America contributed more than 90% of the air forces.
- ☑ 85% of the naval forces were American.

 Why did the USA's response to the invasion of South Korea lead to some people calling it 'America's war'?

Some people called the Korean War *(p.16)* 'America's war' for the following reasons:

- ☑ The amount of troops the USA sent to support UN forces - 302,483 soldiers in total. The UK sent the second highest number of troops, but that was only 14,198.

- [x] An American, General MacArthur, led the UN army in Korea.
- [x] It was widely known the forces took their orders from the USA rather than from the United Nations.

DID YOU KNOW?

The Korean War was the first war to feature battles between jet aircraft.

GENERAL MACARTHUR AND THE KOREAN WAR

'It is fatal to enter any war without the will to win it.' General MacArthur.

 What did General Douglas MacArthur do in the Korean War?

At the age of 70, General Douglas MacArthur was appointed chief of the UN task force sent to Korea in 1950. He played a significant role in the Korean War *(p.16)*.

 What were the key events General Douglas MacArthur was involved in during the Korean War?

The 8 key events of MacArthur's role in the Korean War *(p.16)* included:

- [x] When MacArthur arrived in Korea, his first job was to stop the South Korean army being completely wiped out. He sent troops to defend the area around the city of Pusan.
- [x] MacArthur then launched a surprise attack, called the Inchon Landings.
- [x] Next, he led UN forces to recapture the city of Seoul, which had fallen to Kim Il-Sung's North Korean army.
- [x] By October 1950, MacArthur had successfully led the UN campaign to drive the North Korean army back to their homeland, behind the 38th parallel.
- [x] MacArthur then launched an offensive into North Korea in the hope of reuniting Korea under capitalism. This went against recommendations not to do so, due to the concern China would join the war. However, MacArthur was confident Mao's troops would not attack.
- [x] MacArthur's predictions were wrong, and he and his troops were pushed back into South Korea by the united force of North Korean and Chinese soldiers.
- [x] MacArthur was ordered by Truman not to go back into North Korea. He ignored this, saying he wanted to unite Korea and the USA should be prepared to engage in nuclear warfare if this is what it took.
- [x] As a result of disregarding President Truman's orders, MacArthur was sacked in April 1951 and ordered to return to the USA.

 Why was General Douglas MacArthur sacked during the Korean War?

MacArthur was sacked because he disobeyed direct orders. There was real concern he might trigger a nuclear war. Some people felt he deliberately provoked China into entering the war by ignoring their warnings against advancing further north in Korea. He also repeatedly expressed a willingness to use nuclear weapons.

 Who took over General Douglas MacArthur's role in the Korean War?

General MacArthur was replaced by Lieutenant General Matthew Ridgway.

 What was the public reaction to General Douglas MacArthur being sacked during the Korean War?

MacArthur was a popular war hero in America and his sacking was condemned by the public. He received a hero's welcome on his return home.

What was the significance of General Douglas MacArthur's role during the Korean War?

MacArthur was a significant and controversial figure in the Korean War *(p.16)* for 5 main reasons:

☑ He was responsible for changing the tide of events, masterminding the Inchon Landing, and was able to recapture South Korea at the start of the war.

☑ His actions led to China's involvement, which turned the tide again - but this time not in the UN's favour.

☑ He was sacked by President Truman for disregarding orders and was replaced by Lieutenant General Ridgeway.

☑ His attitude regarding nuclear warfare was heavily criticised. Some people felt there was a real danger of the conflict becoming a nuclear war and MacArthur was pushing towards this.

☑ He wrote a public letter criticising President Truman.

THE SUCCESS OF THE KOREAN WAR

'It will begin with its President taking a simple, firm resolution...to concentrate on the job of ending the war in Korea'.
General Eisenhower, 1952

 How successful was American intervention in Korea?

The Korean War *(p.16)* fulfilled a number of US containment *(p.70)* aims, but at a cost.

 How successful was American intervention in Korea?

The Korean War *(p.16)* was successful from the point of view of the US for a number of reasons.

☑ South Korea remained out of communist hands.

☑ The UN was shown to be more purposeful than the League of Nations had been, in using military sanctions to stop an act of aggression.

☑ It confirmed US policy in Asia and led to the setting up of SEATO.

 How was American intervention in Korea unsuccessful?

The success of the Korean War *(p.16)* was limited by a number of factors.

☑ It was costly in terms of life and money. The number of Americans who died per year was actually higher than during the Vietnam War.

☑ It failed to liberate North Korea from communism.

☑ It highlighted tension between American leaders, those who wanted to contain and prevent the spread of communism, and those who wanted to push back and win back communist countries.

☑ When China involved itself in the war it became a new major threat for the USA. Even after the fighting had stopped, US soldiers remained stationed in South Korea which irritated the Chinese government and put pressure on relations between the two countries.

☑ It had a devastating impact on the Korean people. Around a 10th of the population died.

DID YOU KNOW?

The Korean War ended on 27th July 1953, with the signing of an armistice, or ceasefire.

However, in 2020 the Korean War had still never been formally ended.

Quizzes, amazing exam preparation tools and more at GCSEHistory.com

AMERICAN INFLUENCE IN CUBA

'We considered it part of the United States practically, just a wonderful little country over there that was of no danger to anybody'.
Walter Cronkite

 ### How did US influence impact on Cuba?

America had had influence on Cuba's government, economy and society since the 19th century.

 ### When did America's influence in Cuba begin?

After the Treaty of Paris in 1898, Cuba gained independence from Spain, but the USA had a right to supervise Cuba's finances and foreign relations.

 ### How did the USA benefit from its influence over Cuba?

The USA benefitted economically from its rights in Cuba in 5 key ways:

- ☑ America forced Cuba to sell raw materials at low prices.
- ☑ The USA also made sure Cuba bought American goods - by 1914, 75% of Cuban imports were American.
- ☑ The USA ran the Cuban railway industry, telephone system and tobacco plantations.
- ☑ Two thirds of all Cuban arable farmland belonged to Americans.
- ☑ America had a naval base at Guantanamo Bay.

 ### What was the problem with US influence in Cuba?

American interference was causing discontent in Cuba by the 1950s in 6 main ways:

- ☑ The USA had a huge influence over Cuban politics, and no Cuban government could be elected unless they were prepared to support American interference.
- ☑ Cuba was a tourist destination for Americans who were interested in activities that were illegal in America, e.g. drinking, gambling and prostitution. This led to more crime.
- ☑ The American Mafia controlled much of the gambling and hotels in Cuba.
- ☑ The Americans supported Batista as president, whose regime murdered over 20,000 Cubans.
- ☑ Many ordinary Cubans were poor and did not have sufficient education or healthcare.
- ☑ There was segregation of black and white people, as in America.

DID YOU KNOW?

When he fled Cuba, Batista is said to have taken his personal funds of $300 million.

THE CUBAN REVOLUTION

'A revolution is a struggle to the death between the future and the past'.
Fidel Castro

 ### What was the Cuban Revolution?

Fidel Castro led an armed uprising to bring down the dictatorship of the Cuban president, General Fulgencio Batista.

When was the Cuban Revolution?

The Cuban Revolution started in July 1953. Batista was removed from power on 31st December, 1958.

 ## Who started the Cuban Revolution?

Fidel Castro started the Cuban Revolution.

 ## How did the Cuban Revolution affect Cuba's relationship with the USA?

Before 1959, the USA supported Batista and there was co-operation between the two countries. This ended when diplomatic relations were broken off in January 1961.

 ## What was the USA's reaction to the Cuban Revolution?

The USA reacted in 7 key ways:

- ✅ It wanted Cuba back inside America's sphere of influence.
- ✅ In 1959, it refused to accept compensation offered by Cuba for American-owned property and land taken in the revolution.
- ✅ Although America did recognise Castro's government, when he requested economic aid in 1960 this was denied. Instead, President Eisenhower reduced US imports of Cuban sugar by 95%.
- ✅ It supported Cuban exiles to undermine the new government.
- ✅ It refused to buy Cuban sugar, which made up a large part of the national income, and eventually ended all trade with Cuba in October 1960.
- ✅ The CIA tried unsuccessfully to assassinate Castro.
- ✅ The CIA convinced President Kennedy that the USA needed to invade Cuba.

 ## What became of Cuba's relationship with the USSR after the Cuban Revolution?

There were 3 important developments in Cuba's relationship with the Soviet Union:

- ✅ Cuba began to build economic links with the Soviet Union instead of the USA.
- ✅ In February 1960, it began to trade Cuban sugar for Soviet oil.
- ✅ Cuba wanted the Soviets' military defence and support.

DID YOU KNOW?

Castro's signature beard was a symbol of the months that he had spent in hiding as a revolutionary, and was seen as a mark of honour.

Apparently, the CIA considered a plot to make it fall out with thallium salts, as a way of undermining his popularity.

Quizzes, amazing exam preparation tools and more at GCSEHistory.com

FIDEL CASTRO

'It does not matter how small you are if you have faith and a plan of action'.
Fidel Castro

Who was Castro?

Fidel Castro was a wealthy Cuban who trained as a lawyer. He was a revolutionary and nationalist who became the communist leader of Cuba.

How did Castro take over Cuba?

Castro organised a revolutionary group called the 26th of July Movement to overthrow the US-backed Cuban government.

When did Castro overthrow the government of Cuba?

Fidel Castro led a guerrilla force to overthrow the US-backed dictator, President Batista, in 1959.

When did Castro rule Cuba?

Castro was Prime Minister of Cuba from 1959 to 1976, although he led the country until his death in 2016.

What were Castro's ideas?

Castro promised to restore power to the Cuban people and to end American corruption in the country.

How did Castro change industry?

After 1959, Castro introduced 3 important changes to the Cuban economy.

- ☑ He nationalised the telephone industry, so that it was cheaper.
- ☑ He cut rents for low earners by up to 50%.
- ☑ He nationalised land that was owned by foreigners and redistributed it back to Cuban peasants.

How did Castro change education?

Castro made free education available to everyone, and encouraged students to travel to the countryside and teach people to read.

How did Castro change healthcare?

Castro built new training schools for doctors, redistributed doctors from wealthy Havana to other parts of the country, and provided free healthcare for all Cubans.

How did Castro change Cuba's international relations?

Castro negotiated trade agreements with communist countries such as the USSR to sell goods such as sugar in return for weapons.

How did Castro control politics?

About 90% of the population supported Castro, although he never held free elections and he imprisoned and exiled people who disagreed with him.

How did Castro change Cuban society?

Fidel Castro ended the segregation of facilities such as beaches and hotels for different racial groups.

Who opposed Fidel Castro?

90% of the Cuban population supported Castro, but he had 2 important opponents and critics.

☑ Members of Batista's regime were exiled to America and put pressure on the government there to depose Castro.

☑ Americans were angry about losing their land and industries to nationalisation.

 What role did Fidel Castro play in the Cold War?

Castro was in power during the Bay of Pigs Crisis and the Cuban Missile Crisis *(p.29)*. Relations between America and Cuba deteriorated during this time.

DID YOU KNOW?

The CIA considered several different plans to assassinate Castro.

These included poisoning his cigars, diving suit and pens, and planting an explosive seashell.

THE BAY OF PIGS, 1961

'On that unhappy island, as in so many other areas of the contest for freedom, the news has grown worse instead of better'.
John F Kennedy, April 1961

 What happened at the Bay of Pigs in Cuba?

The Bay of Pigs incident involved Cuban exiles, supported by US forces, invading Cuba.

 When was the attack at the Bay of Pigs?

The invasion of Cuba at the Bay of Pigs took place on 17th April, 1961.

 What happened during the invasion of the Bay of Pigs?

There were 4 key events during the invasion of the Bay of Pigs:

☑ Castro learned about the invasion in advance because the planes were recognised as American from photographs.

☑ The 1,400 US-backed Cuban exiles were met by an army of 20,000 Cubans.

☑ The US-backed Cuban exiles surrendered.

☑ Almost all of those in the Cuban exile army were jailed or shot.

 What were the consequences of the attack at the Bay of Pigs?

There were 5 important consequences of the attack at the Bay of Pigs:

☑ The incident meant USA-Cuban relations deteriorated while Soviet-Cuban relations improved.

☑ Fidel Castro stayed in power.

☑ The USA was totally discredited because it had supported illegal acts. President Kennedy was embarrassed and his position was weakened.

☑ In December 1961, Castro stated he and his government were communist.

☑ Castro asked Khrushchev *(p.32)* for military support in case of future attacks by the USA.

Why did the invasion at the Bay of Pigs fail?

There were 2 main reasons why the invasion at the Bay of Pigs failed:

☑ The CIA underestimated the strength of the Cubans, who had 20,000 troops and modern tanks and weapons.

☑ They also failed to gain the support of the Cuban people, which they assumed they would get.

DID YOU KNOW?

The American B-26s used in the Bay of Pigs invasion were an hour late.

This was probably because there was confusion over the different time zone in Cuba.

THE CUBAN MISSILE CRISIS, 1962

'We're eyeball to eyeball…and I think the other fellow just blinked.'
Secretary of State Dean Rusk, October 1962

 What was the Cuban Missile Crisis?

The Cuban Missile Crisis, between the USSR and the USA, was one of the most serious Cold War crises. It happened because the USSR placed missiles in Cuba and was the closest the world had been to a possible nuclear war.

 When did the Cuban Missile Crisis happen?

The Cuban Missile Crisis lasted for 13 days, from 14th to 28th October, 1962.

 Why did the Cuban Missile Crisis happen?

6 important causes of the Cuban Missile Crisis were:

☑ The long-term deterioration of the relationship between the USA and Cuba, accelerated by the Cuban Revolution *(p.25)* in 1959 and the Bay of Pigs incident in 1961.

☑ This pushed Cuba closer to the USSR, which bought Cuban sugar. In return, the Cubans bought oil from the Soviets.

☑ Castro had declared himself a Marxist in December 1961.

☑ Khrushchev *(p.32)* was concerned about the missile gap and the fact the USA had nuclear missiles based in Turkey which could easily reach the USSR.

☑ The immediate cause was the deployment of Soviet nuclear missiles to Cuba for protection against possible attack by the USA.

☑ Cuba is only 160km south of the US state of Florida, which meant the mainland was within range of any missiles placed on Cuba. The USA therefore felt threatened.

 What happened during the Cuban Missile Crisis?

There were 9 key events during the crisis in October 1962:

☑ On 14th October, American spy planes spotted missile bases being built on Cuba.

☑ On 16th October, Kennedy was informed of the missile build-up and Ex-Comm, an advisory group, was formed.

☑ On 20th October, Kennedy decided to blockade Cuba. This was a 500-mile naval 'quarantine' with the aim of preventing the Soviets bringing in further military supplies or missiles.

☑ On 24th October, Khrushchev *(p.32)* stated the USSR would launch nuclear missiles if America went to war in Cuba.

- ✅ The blockade began. When Soviet ships approached the blockade, some stopped and some turned around.
- ✅ On 26th October, Kennedy received a letter from Khrushchev *(p.32)* who offered to negotiate if the blockade was removed and the USA did not invade Cuba.
- ✅ On 27th October, Kennedy received a second letter from Khrushchev *(p.32)* which offered to remove the missiles if the USA removed its missiles in Turkey.
- ✅ Kennedy's brother, Robert, negotiated with the Russian ambassador and accepted the offer on condition the removal of missiles from Turkey was kept secret.
- ✅ On 28th October, Khrushchev *(p.32)* agreed to the dismantling of the nuclear missiles.

How was the Cuban Missile Crisis solved?

The Cuban Missile Crisis was solved because:

- ✅ Khrushchev *(p.32)* agreed to remove missiles from Cuba if the USA removed its warheads from Italy and Turkey.
- ✅ The USA would only agree to the deal if the removal of its missiles from Italy and Turkey was kept secret.

What were the results of the Cuban Missile Crisis?

There were 6 main consequences to the Cuban Missile Crisis:

- ✅ Cuba survived as a communist country.
- ✅ Kennedy assured the world that the USA would never invade Cuba and his public image improved.
- ✅ The Soviet Union looked weak because the world did not know the USA had removed its missiles from Turkey.
- ✅ Khrushchev *(p.32)* lost power in the USSR and was dismissed in 1964.
- ✅ China criticised the USSR over its actions because the Soviets had made the communist world look weak. China's relationship with the USSR deteriorated.
- ✅ The USA's NATO allies in Europe were horrified because they had not been consulted. France reacted by leaving NATO in 1966.

How did the Cuban Missile Crisis affect the relationship between the USA and the USSR?

The Cuban Missile Crisis had 2 main effects on the relationship between the USA and the USSR:

- ✅ The relationship had deteriorated almost to the brink of nuclear war, so Kennedy wanted to focus more on the two nations' 'common interests'.
- ✅ A hotline *(p.31)* was set up in June 1963 between the USA and the USSR. This would help avoid crises by enabling direct and quick communication.

Why was the Cuban Missile Crisis important?

The Cuban Missile Crisis was important for 2 main reasons:

- ✅ It was the most dangerous Cold War confrontation between the USA and the USSR and almost led to nuclear war.
- ✅ It resulted in both countries working to improve their relationship and slow down the arms race.

What nuclear treaties were signed after The Cuban Missile Crisis?

There were 3 important nuclear treaties signed after the Cuban Missile Crisis:

- ✅ 1963 - the Limited Test Ban Treaty banned the testing of nuclear weapons in air or underwater.
- ✅ 1967 - the Outer Space Treaty banned testing or using nuclear weapons in space.
- ✅ 1968 - the Nuclear Non-Proliferation Treaty stated the ultimate goal was world nuclear disarmament.

THE WASHINGTON - MOSCOW HOTLINE

'Must a world be lost for want of a telephone call?'
Jess Gorkin, 1960

What was the hotline?

The hotline was a teleprinter set up between Washington in the USA and Moscow in the USSR as a way of providing direct communication between the White House and the Kremlin.

When was the hotline set up?

The hotline was set up in June 1963.

Why was the hotline set up?

The hotline was set up as a result of the 1962 Cuban Missile Crisis *(p.29)*. Leaders of the USA and the USSR had been unable to communicate directly during the crisis, relying on letters and messages.

Why was the hotline important?

The hotline was important for 2 main reasons:

- ☑ It meant the USA and USSR could directly communicate with each other so in a crisis they would hopefully solve the issue more quickly.
- ☑ It was a sign that the two superpowers were attempting to improve their relationship.

HOW SUCCESSFUL WAS THE USA IN CUBA?

'I believe that, without being aware of it, we conceived and created the Castro movement, starting from scratch'.
John F Kennedy, 1963

How successfully did the USA contain communism in Cuba?

Historians debate whether communism was contained successfully in Cuba.

How did the US successfully contain communism in Cuba?

The US prevented nuclear missiles from being placed on Cuba.

 How did the US fail in containing communism in Cuba?

Cuba remained communist.

DID YOU KNOW?

The American nuclear PGM-19 Jupiter missiles in Turkey were already mostly obsolete by the time of the Cuban Missile Crisis.

WHICH LEADER WAS THE MOST SUCCESSFUL IN THE CUBAN MISSILE CRISIS?

'If he thinks I'm inexperienced and have no guts, until we remove those ideas we won't get anywhere with him'.
JFK on Khrushchev, 1959

 What leader was most successful in the Cuban Missile Crisis?

Historians debate whether Kennedy or Khrushchev was more successful at dealing with the Cuban Missile Crisis *(p.29)*.

 How successful was Kennedy at dealing with the Cuban Missile Crisis?

Some historians argue that Kennedy, compared to Khrushchev, dealt more successfully with the Cuban Missile Crisis *(p.29)*, giving 2 key reasons.

☑ Kennedy was seen as strong and decisive and his popularity soared.

☑ Kennedy had successfully prevented nuclear missiles from being placed on Cuba.

 How successful was Khrushchev at dealing with the Cuban Missile Crisis?

Some historians argue that Khrushchev, compared to Kennedy, had more success with the Cuban Missile crisis *(p.29)*, giving 4 key reasons.

☑ Khrushchev had prevented a nuclear war by agreeing to compromise.

☑ The USA had agreed not to invade Cuba, so the USSR still had a communist ally close to America.

☑ As Cuba remained communist, the US policy of containment *(p.70)* had failed.

DID YOU KNOW?

Khrushchev visited the USA in 1959.

His scheduled visit to Disneyland had to be cancelled for security reasons and he was very upset.

FRENCH RULE IN VIETNAM

'A poor feudal nation had beaten a great colonial power'.
Vietminh commander Vo Nguyen Giap

 Who controlled Vietnam before the Second World War?

France fully took over Indochina in the late 19th century. France lost control to the Japanese during the Second World War, but wanted to regain it in 1945.

 Who supported French rule in Vietnam?

French rule in Vietnam was supported by the USA, under President Truman, after March 1945. They provided around $500 million a year in support.

 Why did the USA support French rule in Vietnam?

The US wanted to prevent communism spreading in Asia, particularly after the fall of China to communism in 1949.

 Who challenged French rule in Vietnam?

French rule in Vietnam was challenged by the Vietminh, a Vietnamese resistance movement founded to fight the Japanese during the Second World War. It was led by the communist Ho Chi Minh *(p.39)*.

 How was French rule in Vietnam defeated?

The Vietminh used guerrilla warfare to defeat the French.

 What were the reasons for the defeat of French rule in Vietnam?

There were 6 main reasons why the French were defeated in Vietnam.

- ☑ The Vietminh were able to use their excellent geographical knowledge to their advantage, using it to launch surprise attacks on the French.
- ☑ The Vietminh were aided by China and the USSR, who sent troops and supplies.
- ☑ Villagers supported the Vietminh, by spying and deploying supplies.
- ☑ The Vietminh used guerrilla warfare.
- ☑ The French troops did not care about regaining control of Vietnam. France also underestimated the Vietminh.
- ☑ There was limited assistance from the US.

 When did the French rule end in Vietnam?

The French left Vietnam in July 1956.

DID YOU KNOW?

The name is Nguyen is used by up to an estimated 40% of the Vietnamese population.

This was because it was assigned to many people by the French, who discovered that many Vietnamese didn't have a family name during their rule, and gave them the name of the last Vietnamese monarchy.

THE BATTLE OF DIEN BIEN PHU

'An unfortunate accident'.
French officer on the Battle of Dien Bien Phu

What was Dien Bien Phu?

Dien Bien Phu was a decisive battle between French and North Vietnamese troops in 1954.

When did Dien Bien Phu take place?

The Battle of Dien Bien Phu was fought for 57 days between 13th March and 7th May, 1954.

Who was involved at Dien Bien Phu?

France fought the Battle of Dien Bien Phu against North Vietnam and the Vietminh.

What was the result of Dien Bien Phu?

There were 5 significant results of Dien Bien Phu.

- ☑ France lost the battle.
- ☑ Over 3,000 French soldiers were killed and 8,000 were wounded.
- ☑ The Vietminh lost 8,000 troops and a further 12,000 were wounded.
- ☑ It was a massive humiliation for the French.
- ☑ The remaining French soldiers were made to march to prisons located far away, with many dying during the journey.

Why did Dien Bien Phu happen?

The French felt one last large battle would defeat the communists.

How were the French defeated at Dien Bien Phu?

The French were defeated for 6 main reasons:

- ☑ The 10,000 French soldiers defended an airfield known as Dien Bien Phu, which was in a valley.
- ☑ The French were surrounded and had their supplies cut off by 50,000 Vietminh soldiers.
- ☑ The Vietnamese were willing to use suicide bombers.
- ☑ The Vietnamese managed to get artillery to the top of the surrounding hills and bombarded Dien Bien Phu.
- ☑ They launched attacks with vast numbers of men and were willing to take heavy casualties.
- ☑ The French ran out of essential supplies like water and medicines. Although they asked for help, neither the USA nor Britain would come to their aid. The French surrendered on 7th May, 1954.

Why did the French surrender at Dien Bien Phu?

The French surrendered at Dien Bien Phu for 3 key reasons:

- ☑ They had been defeated in the battle.
- ☑ They could not secure support from outside parties such as Britain and the USA.
- ☑ The French parliament voted 471 to 14 in support of ending the war and withdrawing from French Indochina.

What were the consequences of Dien Bien Phu?

The defeat at Dien Bien Phu had 2 important consequences.

- ☑ It ended France's 8-year war with the Vietminh.
- ☑ Over 400,000 soldiers and civilians lost their lives in the First Indochina War.

> **DID YOU KNOW?**
>
> **At the Battle of Dien Bien Phu, troops wearing sandals made out of old rubber tyres were led by General Vo Nguyen Giap.**
>
> These sandals were known as 'Uncle Ho' sandals, because they were a favourite of Ho Chi Minh.

THE DOMINO THEORY

'You have a row of dominoes set up, you knock over the first one, and what will happen to the last one is the certainty that it will go over very quickly'.
President Dwight Eisenhower, 1954

What was the Domino Theory?

The Domino Theory said that if one country fell under communist influence, the surrounding nations in that region would also fall - like a line of dominos.

When was the Domino Theory created?

The phrase 'Domino Theory' was first used in 1954.

Who came up with the Domino Theory?

The phrase was first used by US President Eisenhower when he suggested the fall of French Indochina to communism could result in a domino effect in south east Asia.

What started the idea of the Domino Theory?

The idea of the 'Domino Theory' was a consequence of the Cold War. The 3 main causes were:

- ☑ The US government had committed to limiting the spread of communism in Europe through the Marshall Plan. The idea was that communism would take root in poorer countries, so supporting those nations' economies would stop the spread.

- ☑ The USA witnessed communist takeovers in some Asian countries including China, North Korea, and North Vietnam.

- ☑ Eisenhower believed Ho Chi Minh *(p.39)* wanted all of Vietnam to become communist, and that if this happened communism would spread to Laos, Cambodia, Thailand, Burma, Malaysia, Indonesia and India. Vietnam was the first 'domino'.

What was a consequence of the Domino Theory?

To stop the spread of communism in south-east Asia President Eisenhower set up the Southeast Asia Treaty Organization (SEATO) with seven other countries in 1954.

What was the impact of the Domino Theory on the USA?

The fear triggered by the Domino Theory impacted the USA in 5 key ways:

- ☑ People began to believe there were Soviet spies living among American people and plotting to overthrow the government.

- ☑ The House Un-American Activities Committee (HUAC) was established to investigate suspected communist spies.

- ☑ Some filmmakers were accused of spreading communist propaganda.

- ☑ The McCarran Act was passed. This legislation restricted employment for communists and stipulated that all communist organisations had to be registered and investigated.
- ☑ It led to something called the Red Scare, a paranoia about communism, which facilitated McCarthyism. This in turn led to an increase of public support for greater involvement in Vietnam.

DID YOU KNOW?

President Dwight Eisenhower, who popularised the Domino Theory in 1954, was the first president to ride in a helicopter.

THE GENEVA ACCORDS, 1954

'IT was generally agreed that had an election been held, Ho Chi Minh would have been elected Premier...'
President Eisenhower

What were the Geneva Accords?

The Geneva Conference was a meeting between 9 countries which focused on resolving the war between France and the Democratic Republic of Vietnam. The agreements that were reached became known as the Geneva Accords.

When was the Geneva Conference?

The Geneva Conference took place from 26th April to 21st July, 1954.

Who attended the Geneva Conference?

Representatives of 9 countries attended the Geneva Conference:

- ☑ Cambodia.
- ☑ Laos.
- ☑ China.
- ☑ France.
- ☑ Britain.
- ☑ USSR.
- ☑ USA.
- ☑ Vietminh (North Vietnam).
- ☑ The State of Vietnam (South Vietnam).

Where was the Geneva Conference held?

The conference was held in Geneva, Switzerland.

Why was the Geneva Conference held?

The Geneva Conference was held to bring a peaceful end to the conflict in Indochina.

What was agreed by the Geneva Accords?

The Geneva Accords resulted in numerous important agreements regarding Vietnam:

- ✅ Vietnam was split into two on a temporary basis, with a demilitarised zone in the middle. The country was divided at the 17th parallel, which was approximately halfway down.
- ✅ The south would be run by Emperor Bao Dai, who had spent a lot of time in the USA and strongly opposed communism.
- ✅ The north would be controlled by Ho Chi Minh *(p.39)*, a communist.
- ✅ France had to withdraw from Vietnam.
- ✅ The Vietminh had to withdraw from the south.
- ✅ The Vietnamese could choose if they wanted to live in the north or the south.
- ✅ Elections were to be held in 1956 to decide who ruled the whole of Vietnam. However, no clear electoral system was agreed.
- ✅ No foreign forces would be allowed to set up military bases in Vietnam.
- ✅ There were 300 days of free movement. One million people moved south; 130,000 moved north; and 5,000 to 10,000 supporters of North Vietnam stayed in the south.
- ✅ Laos and Cambodia were created.

What was the USA's response to the Geneva Accords?

President Eisenhower was worried about the spread of communism in the region and was committed to containing it. The USA refused to sign the accords, but became more involved in the future of Vietnam. In January 1955, America sent a shipment of military aid to Saigon, the capital of South Vietnam, and offered to train the new army.

What was the response of South Vietnam to the Geneva Accords?

South Vietnam refused to sign the accords. Diem *(p.37)*, the prime minister, did not want to accept the division of the country as he wanted a united Vietnam.

What was the response of North Vietnam to the Geneva Accords?

China forced North Vietnam to agree to the demands, even though it would have a smaller area of control than in 1945. Ho Chi Minh *(p.39)* wanted a united country, but he believed the division would only be temporary as the people of Vietnam would vote for a communist government in the elections that were due to be held before July 1956.

DID YOU KNOW?

The Geneva Convention had originally been planned to discuss Korea and Cuba, but the Battle of Dien Bien Phu forced Vietnam onto the agenda.

NGO DINH DIEM

'We know of no-one better'
JP Dulles

Who was Ngo Dinh Diem?

Ngo Dinh Diem was the final prime minister of the State of Vietnam from 1954 to 1955, and then President of South Vietnam from 1955 to 1963.

Who led South Vietnam before Ngo Dinh Diem?

The leader of South Vietnam before Ngo Dinh Diem was Bao Dai, a former emperor of Vietnam, who led anti-communist forces in South Vietnam after the departure of the French.

Was Diem a good president?

Diem was initially regarded as a good president. He built new schools and strengthened the economy. However, this changed because he increased his power, allowed corruption, and was anti-Buddhist.

 What were the reasons Diem lacked support?

Diem lacked support for 6 important reasons:

- ☑ Most of the South Vietnamese population was Buddhist, but Diem favoured Catholics and gave them government jobs.
- ☑ There were still a lot of communists in South Vietnam who opposed him.
- ☑ A number of other political and religious groups used their own armies to oppose Diem.
- ☑ Diem showed little respect for the villages, or for anyone who lived outside Saigon.
- ☑ When villagers complained about greedy and corrupt landowners, he did nothing to help them.
- ☑ His promised land reforms failed.

 How did Diem deal with his opponents?

Diem ordered the arrest of those who opposed him, and those who were suspected of being communists. It is estimated there were 65,000 arrests, and that 2,000 people were killed.

 How did Diem break the Geneva Accords?

Under the Geneva Accords, there were supposed to be elections in 1956, but Diem refused to hold them.

 Who supported Diem?

Diem had support from the USA, which was concerned the proposed 1956 elections would be won by the communists.

 How did the USA support Diem?

Advisers were sent by President Eisenhower to train the Army of the Republic of Vietnam - the ARVN.

 Why did the USA support Diem?

The USA remained in Vietnam after the Geneva Accords for 2 main reasons.

- ☑ President Diem's government was not strong or popular enough.
- ☑ President Eisenhower believed in the Domino Theory *(p.35)*, and was concerned about the spread of communism in Southeast Asia.

DID YOU KNOW?

Ngo Dinh Diem's brother and sister-in-law, Ngo Dinh Nhu and Madame Nhu, were especially hated in South Vietnam.

Ngo Dinh Nhu was the head of the Can Lao, the South Vietnamese secret police, which used terror tactics to control the population.

HO CHI MINH

'It was patriotism, not communism, that inspired me'.
Ho Chi Minh

 Who was Ho Chi Minh?

Ho Chi Minh was the communist leader of North Vietnam.

 What does Ho Chi Minh's name mean?

Ho Chi Minh means 'Enlightened One'.

 What were Ho Chi Minh's main aims?

Ho Chi Minh's main aim was to achieve a communist, united, and independent Vietnam.

 What were Ho Chi Minh's achievements?

Ho Chi Minh had 8 main achievements including:

- ☑ He founded the Vietminh.
- ☑ He led the Vietnamese to victory over the Japanese and the French, and played a major role in the war against the US.
- ☑ He helped communism to develop in Vietnam.
- ☑ He was instrumental in the development of the Ho Chi Minh Trail.
- ☑ He was prime minister of North Vietnam from 1945 to 1955.
- ☑ He was president of North Vietnam from 1945 to 1969.
- ☑ He created the North Vietnamese Army and the Vietcong *(p.39)*.
- ☑ He established links with China and the USSR.

 What was Ho Chi Minh's link to the Vietcong?

He was instrumental in the creation of the Vietcong *(p.39)* by encouraging the different armed groups in the south to work together as one organisation. The new organisation became known as the National Liberation Front in December 1960. In the south they were called the 'Vietcong' which meant Vietnamese communist.

DID YOU KNOW?

Ho Chi Minh was originally named Nguyen Tat Thanh.

THE DEVELOPMENT OF THE VIETCONG

'You will kill ten of us, we will kill one of you, but in the end, you will tire of it first.'
Ho Chi Minh

 What was the Vietcong?

The Vietcong (VC) was made up of over a dozen different political and religious groups based in South Vietnam. They opposed the South Vietnamese government, both politically and militarily.

When was the Vietcong established?

The Vietcong was established on 20th December, 1960.

 Who was the leader of the Vietcong?

The leader of the Vietcong was Hua Tho. Although he was non-communist, so were many members of the organisation.

 Why was the Vietcong established?

The Vietcong was formed for three main reasons:

☑ There was much anger and frustration at Diem's *(p.37)* failure to hold the elections agreed at the Geneva Conference, which would have meant a united Vietnam.

☑ Frustration pushed some people to violence, and groups of South Vietnamese people intended to use terror tactics to force elections or overthrow Diem's *(p.43)* regime.

☑ The violence resulted in many members of Diem's *(p.37)* government being murdered. He hit back by sending the ARVN into the jungle to hunt down rebel forces. A report produced by Ho Chi Minh's *(p.39)* advisor, Le Duan, commented that Diem's policy was proving successful, and therefore the rebel forces in South Vietnam had to become more organised.

 What was Ho Chi Minh's involvement with the Vietcong?

Le Duan's report convinced Ho Chi Minh *(p.39)* that he needed to help the resistance fighters in the south if they were to be successful. He persuaded different armed groups who opposed Diem *(p.37)* to come together in one organisation - the National Liberation Front, or the Vietcong, as it was called by the ARVN and US advisers.

 What were the aims of the Vietcong?

The Vietcong had 3 key aims.

☑ It wanted to overthrow Diem *(p.43)* and establish a new government that represented all groups in South Vietnamese society.

☑ It was committed to the reunification of Vietnam, independent of all foreign influence.

☑ It was committed to the redistribution of wealth and restoration of peasants' rights.

 Who supported the Vietcong?

The Vietcong had both domestic and international support.

☑ Domestic support for the Vietcong was vast. As well as communists, and nationalists who wanted reunification, it appealed to the middle classes, teachers, doctors, and also peasants and workers.

☑ Internationally, the Vietcong was supported by North Vietnam, China and the USSR.

 How was the Vietcong supported by the North?

The North developed various supply routes to help the Vietcong, including the Ho Chi Minh Trail.

 How did the Vietcong fight?

The Vietcong used 4 guerrilla tactics against Diem's *(p.37)* ARVN forces.

☑ Their aim was not to destroy, but to wear down.

☑ They fought in cells of 8-10 soldiers.

☑ They blended into the population, making it difficult for Diem's *(p.37)* forces to find them.

☑ They picked their battles, attacking at night and only fighting if they outnumbered enemy soldiers.

What was the difference between the Vietcong and the Vietminh?

The Vietminh was the anti-Japanese and anti-French force created in the 1940s to drive out foreign colonialists. After the division of Vietnam, its members resided in the north. The Vietcong was created in the 1950s to fight Diem's *(p.37)* regime in the south, and was used as North Vietnam's vehicle for creating chaos across the south.

 What did the Vietcong do to gain help and support?

The Vietcong used both positive and oppressive methods to control the Vietnamese.

☑ They used violence and intimidation to control villages.

☑ They created a political group called the National Liberation Front (NLF). It spread communist ideas among the villages, and encouraged people to help the Vietcong.

 How did President Kennedy try to defeat the Vietcong?

President Kennedy sent an extra 16,000 advisers to South Vietnam, to train the Army of the Republic of Vietnam (ARVN) to fight the Vietcong. They were called 'advisers' rather than troops, because he wanted to avoid full-scale war.

 What were President Kennedy's motives towards the Vietcong?

President Kennedy wanted to stop communism and destroy the Vietcong.

 Why did President Kennedy fail to defeat the Vietcong?

President Kennedy's attempt to defeat the Vietcong failed for 3 main reasons:

☑ Efforts by US troops to train villagers to fight the Vietcong were unsuccessful because the Americans could not speak Vietnamese.

☑ The US troops were unable to stop the Vietcong visiting the villages at night, once they had left.

☑ The USA supported the ARVN, which was regarded as part of Diem's *(p.37)* corrupt government.

 Why did the USA see the Vietcong as a threat?

The Vietcong was seen as a threat by the USA for 5 significant reasons:

☑ Although the ARVN had five times as many troops, it was too concerned over who should lead rather than pulling together to defeat the Vietcong.

☑ China supported the Vietcong by using the Ho Chi Minh Trail to send $100 million in aid to South Vietnam.

☑ The South Vietnamese government was seen as the USA's puppet and remained unpopular.

☑ The introduction of reforms, and the use of propaganda, meant the Vietcong gained local support.

☑ The number of attacks by the Vietcong increased and were focused on US military targets.

 What was President Johnson's response to the Vietcong threat?

After President Kennedy was assassinated, President Johnson increased the number of US advisers in South Vietnam to 20,000. He wanted to avoid US involvement in an escalating war by ensuring the establishment of a democratic and popular government that would oppose communism.

 How did the Vietcong react to US intervention?

In the early 1960s, the Vietcong began 2 main projects to counter increasing US intervention:

☑ The amount of supplies brought along the Ho Chi Minh Trail was increased.

☑ It increased the number of guerrilla attacks, from 50 in September, 1961, to 150 in October.

Why did the Vietcong become more dangerous to the USA?

There were 3 main reasons why the Vietcong threat increased:

☑ Increasing tensions with the Americans had pushed the Vietcong to use more violent methods.

☑ America was increasing supplies, troops and operations in South Vietnam.

☑ However, the South Vietnamese were still unable to hold elections.

DID YOU KNOW?

The US personnel referred to the Vietcong as 'Charlie'.

This was because they were known as V.C. which in the phonetic alphabet is pronounced as Victor-Charlie.

THE STRATEGIC HAMLET PROGRAMME

'Peasants resented working without pay to dig moats, implant bamboo stakes, and erect fences against an enemy that did not threaten them...'
An observer in South Vietnam

 What was the Strategic Hamlet programme?

The Strategic Hamlet programme was an initiative introduced by Diem *(p.37)*, supported by President Kennedy and the US government that saw around 5,000 new villages built in South Vietnam.

 When was the Strategic Hamlet programme introduced?

The Strategic Hamlet programme began in March 1962.

 Why was the Strategic Hamlet programme introduced?

There were 3 key reasons the programme was introduced.

☑ Diem *(p.37)* was a very unpopular leader and it was an attempt to 'win the hearts and minds' of the South Vietnamese population.

☑ Diem *(p.37)* portrayed it as a policy that helped the South Vietnamese people defend themselves against the Vietcong *(p.39)*.

☑ The hidden reason for the programme was to stop the Vietcong *(p.39)* using peasant villages for food and shelter. They also wanted to stop the Vietcong from gathering intelligence about the ARVN from the peasants.

 How did the Strategic Hamlet programme work?

The programme worked by moving peasants away from their homes to new villages known as 'strategic hamlets'. These were surrounded by ditches and barbed wire. In just one year, between 1962 and 1963, two thirds of South Vietnamese people were forced to live in strategic hamlets.

 How did the USA hope to gain support with the Strategic Hamlet programme?

It was hoped measures such as building new schools and hospitals, as part of the Strategic Hamlet programme, would build strong support for Diem *(p.37)*.

Why did the Strategic Hamlet programme fail?

The Strategic Hamlet programme failed for 4 key reasons:

- ☑ The new villages needed inhabitants, so people were forced to move into them even if they didn't want to.
- ☑ Many villagers believed they should live where their ancestors were buried, so the move upset them for religious reasons.
- ☑ Other peasants did not want to have to travel further to reach their rice fields.
- ☑ Not enough food was provided by the government, which meant some of those in the new hamlets faced starvation.

 What were the consequences of the Strategic Hamlet programme?

The Strategic Hamlet programme had two key consequences:

- ☑ The programme made people less likely to support Diem *(p.37)*, not more. Membership of the National Liberation Front and the Vietcong *(p.39)* increased by 300% in two years.
- ☑ Its failure led Kennedy to increase the USA's involvement in Vietnam, and he sent more military advisors to support Diem *(p.37)* and the ARVN.

 What was the role of the Strategic Hamlet programme in the Hearts and Minds initiative?

'Hearts and Minds' was an American pacification programme, designed to persuade the South Vietnamese to reject communism. The Strategic Hamlets Programme was one aspect of it.

DID YOU KNOW?

By September 1962, an estimated 4.3 million South Vietnamese were living in Strategic Hamlets.

THE OVERTHROW OF DIEM

'Follow me if I advance! Kill me if I retreat! Revenge me if I die!'
Ngo Dinh Diem

 What led to the overthrow of the Diem government?

Diem's *(p.37)* government became increasingly unpopular.

 What were the events that led to the overthrow of the Diem government?

The overthrow of the Diem government was the result of 4 key events:

- ☑ The loss of the Battle of Ap Bac, despite enormous support from the US military.
- ☑ In May 1963, Diem's *(p.37)* troops opened fire on a Buddhist procession and killed nine people.
- ☑ In June 1963, a Buddhist monk named Thich Quang Duc burned himself to death in Saigon as a protest against Diem's *(p.37)* treatment of Buddhists. Diem responded by ordering Buddhist temples to be raided and closed.
- ☑ America announced publicly it would no longer support Diem *(p.37)* and his government.

 What was the result of the overthrow of the Diem government?

Diem *(p.37)* was removed from power by ARVN generals and later assassinated.

How was the USA involved in the overthrow of the Diem government?

While the USA was not directly involved with Diem's *(p.37)* assassination, there was evidence it was aware of the plot and made no move to prevent it due to Diem's unpopularity and instability.

Who took over after Diem was overthrown?

After Diem *(p.37)* was removed from power, South Vietnam was ruled by a series of military leaders until Nguyen Van Thieu became president in 1967.

DID YOU KNOW?

It is still unclear exactly who murdered Diem and his brother, and why.

THE TONKIN GULF

'I do not want to be the first President to lose a war'.
Lyndon B Johnson

What was the Gulf of Tonkin Incident?

The Gulf of Tonkin incident occurred when three North Vietnamese torpedo boats fired on the USS Maddox, an American warship.

When was the Gulf of Tonkin Incident?

The Gulf of Tonkin incident happened on 2nd August, 1964.

Where did the Gulf of Tonkin Incident happen?

It happened in the Gulf of Tonkin, off the east coast of North Vietnam.

Why did the Gulf of Tonkin Incident happen?

Under Operation Plan 34A, South Vietnamese mercenaries were sent into the north. They were supported by US destroyer naval ships positioned in the Gulf of Tonkin, which were North Vietnamese waters. Ho Chi Minh *(p.39)* was unhappy about this and launched the attack.

What were the key events in the Gulf of Tonkin Incident?

There were a number of key events in the Gulf of Tonkin Incident:

- ✅ The USS Maddox was sent to support the South Vietnamese mercenaries.
- ✅ On 3rd August, 1964, three North Vietnamese torpedo boats travelled towards the Maddox.
- ✅ The Maddox fired at the torpedo boats, which fired back. One torpedo hit but didn't explode.
- ✅ The US jets sank one torpedo ship and damaged the other two.
- ✅ On 4th August there was confusion over further attacks from North Vietnam. However, it was a false alarm; none had taken place.
- ✅ Despite the false alarm, Johnson sanctioned an attack on North Vietnam.

What was the second Gulf of Tonkin incident?

The second incident was an alleged attack on US warships in North Vietnamese seas. It never took place, but was reported as having taken place by the US government.

What was President Johnson's response to the Gulf of Tonkin incident?

President Johnson ordered a US air strike on targets in North Vietnam. Two US planes were shot down, which was the final move that allowed full American intervention in the Vietnam War.

What were the consequences of the Gulf of Tonkin incident?

As a result of the incident, Johnson looked to scale up the USA's involvement in Vietnam. However, he first needed powers to do so, so he asked the US government to pass legislation called the Gulf of Tonkin Resolution.

What was the Gulf of Tonkin Resolution?

On 7th August, 1964, the US Congress passed the Gulf of Tonkin Resolution. This gave President Johnson permission to send troops to Vietnam and initiate further attacks on North Vietnam, without gaining permission from Congress or formally declaring war.

How did the Vietcong react to the Gulf of Tonkin incident?

From November 1964, North Vietnam increased the number of troops and supplies going to South Vietnam. The Vietcong *(p.39)* mounted a successful attack on the US airfield at Pleiku, and won the Battle of Binh Gia.

What actions did the USA take after the Gulf of Tonkin incident?

America sent troops to help the South Vietnam government retain power.

What was the significance of the Gulf of Tonkin incident?

The Gulf of Tonkin incident was significant because it provided the opportunity for the USA to escalate its response in Vietnam. Some historians believe it was just an excuse, and the attacks never happened.

DID YOU KNOW?

Four North Vietnamese were killed in the Gulf of Tonkin Incident, but no Americans were wounded.

THE TACTICS OF THE VIETCONG

'Vietnam is a nasty place to fight. But there are no neat and tidy battlefields in the struggle for freedom; there is no 'good' place to die'.
New York Times Magazine, 1965

What tactics did the Vietcong use?

The US army was one of the largest, strongest, most advanced, and well-equipped armies in the world. In order to beat it, and the ARVN, the Vietcong *(p.39)* had to use local jungle knowledge and guerrilla warfare to overcome their enemies' technology and defeat them.

What guerrilla warfare tactics were used by the Vietcong?

The Vietcong *(p.39)* used 6 main guerrilla warfare tactics to fight the US army and the ARVN:

☑ Soldiers did not wear uniforms, so its members could hide in plain sight among peasants. It was very hard to tell them apart from ordinary civilians.

☑ It had no headquarters and operated in small, well-armed groups, making it difficult to find them.

☑ It repurposed US mines by digging them up and creating booby traps, adding bamboo spikes and crossbows.

☑ It followed the rule of retreating when the enemy attacked, and attacking when the enemy retreated.

☑ It never attacked directly, instead picking off the enemy in ones and twos. Vietcong *(p.39)* members were famous for disappearing quickly into tunnels before the enemy had a chance to react.

☑ It constantly attacked enemy camps.

 What was the aim of the Vietcong tactics of guerrilla warfare?

The aim of guerrilla warfare was to create fear and break down the morale of the US forces.

 What did Ho Chi Minh say about the Vietcong tactics of guerrilla warfare?

Ho Chi Minh *(p.39)* said the following:

☑ 'We must not go in for large-scale battles and big victories, unless we are certain of success.'.

☑ 'The aim of guerrilla warfare is to nibble at the enemy, harass him in such a way that he can neither eat nor sleep in peace, to allow him no rest, to wear him out physically and mentally.'.

☑ 'Wherever the enemy goes, he should be attacked by our guerrillas, stumble on land mines, or be greeted by sniper fire.'.

 What were the typical features of a guerrilla fighter that used Vietcong tactics?

Vietcong *(p.39)* fighters shared a number of typical features and attributes:

☑ They had extensive knowledge of the local jungle which helped them ambush the enemy.

☑ They wore everyday civilian clothes so US forces could not identify them.

☑ They usually carried Soviet AK-47 assault rifles. This was a simple weapon to use but very accurate, and it could weather the watery terrain of the jungle.

☑ They travelled light with small rations of rice, enabling them to move quickly through the jungle.

☑ They would have tools to make 'punji sticks', which they used to make booby traps.

 What was important about the Ho Chi Minh Trail to Vietcong tactics?

The Ho Chi Minh trail was incredibly important. It meant North Vietnam could ensure fighters in the south received regular supplies of weapons, food, and soldiers.

 Why did the Vietcong tactic of using the Ho Chi Minh trail make it difficult for the enemy?

The US forces and the ARVN found the Ho Chi Minh *(p.39)* trails difficult for 2 main reasons:

☑ The trail was well organised. By the end of the war, you could travel the route from North Vietnam to Saigon in six weeks. The trail was 15,000 km long, and both US forces and the ARVN found it hard to overcome the challenges it posed.

☑ The US tried bombing the trail. However, when one section was bombed, the Vietcong *(p.39)* simply used a different section.

What was the idea of 'hanging on the belts' of Americans as a tactic of the Vietcong?

The idea was that the Vietcong *(p.39)* remained close to the enemy and engaged in close-quarter fighting. This helped them carry out surprise attacks and ambushes. As the Vietcong stayed so close it made bombing campaigns more difficult, as the Americans did not want to kill their own soldiers.

How were the tunnels used as a tactic by the Vietcong?

The tunnel system allowed the Vietcong *(p.39)* to move across South Vietnam without being seen, rather than risking being a target from the air. The tunnels were widely used as bases, ambush spots, and hospitals and also helped with the 'hanging on the belts of Americans' tactic.

What were the key features of the tunnels the Vietcong used as a tactic?

There were 3 key features of the tunnel systems:

- ☑ They were complicated systems that ran for over 300km beneath the Vietnamese jungle.
- ☑ They included kitchens, hospitals, sleeping quarters and meeting rooms, as well as storerooms for food, weapons, and explosives.
- ☑ They had various defence measures including hand-detonated mines at the surface, trap doors, air-raid shelters, booby traps, blast walls, false tunnels with booby traps, punji traps, tripwires, and remote smoke outlets.

What was the tactic of booby traps used by the Vietcong?

The Vietcong *(p.39)* used 6 main types of booby traps:

- ☑ Punji sticks.
- ☑ Snake pits.
- ☑ Grenade-in-a-can bombs.
- ☑ Flag bombs.
- ☑ Cartridge traps.
- ☑ 'Bouncing Betty' bombs.

How did the Vietcong use the booby trap punji sticks as a tactic?

The Vietcong *(p.39)* sharpened bamboo stakes, hiding them in shallow pits and covering them with leaves. The stakes would pierce the enemy's boots and sever limbs. Sometimes they smeared the spikes with human excrement to infect the casualty's wounds.

How did the Vietcong use the booby trap snake pits as a tactic?

The Vietcong *(p.39)* guerrillas often carried bamboo pit vipers in their packs, to kill any enemy who searched them. They also tied snakes to bamboo sticks and placed them in their tunnel systems. When the bamboo was released, the snake was freed and would attack the enemy.

How did the Vietcong use the booby trap grenade-in-a-can bombs as a tactic?

Two cans were placed on trees, opposite each other. After removing the safety pins, grenades were placed in the cans. A tripwire was then attached to each grenade. When the wire was tripped by the enemy, the grenades would be pulled out of the cans and explode immediately.

How did the Vietcong use the booby trap flag bombs as a tactic?

US troops often captured enemy flags, so, when the Vietcong *(p.39)* left a base or location it would rig its flags with explosives.

How did the Vietcong use the booby trap cartridge traps as a tactic?

It was hard to detect cartridge traps, which made them terrifying. A cartridge - a round of ammunition - was placed inside bamboo and then put in a shallow hole in the ground. At the bottom of the bamboo was a board and a nail. The weight of the enemy on the cartridge caused the nail to act as a firing pin, shooting the bullet upward into the victim's foot.

 How did the Vietcong use the booby trap 'Bouncing Betty' bombs as a tactic?

These traps would launch into the air when triggered and explode approximately 1m above the ground - at the height of the stomach or genitals.

 How many casualties were caused by the Vietcong's booby trap tactics?

The Vietcong's *(p.39)* traps caused around 19% of US casualties.

 How was the organisation of the Vietcong part of its tactics?

The Vietcong *(p.39)* was organised in small groups called cells. Fighters rarely saw anyone outside their cell, so they couldn't betray the wider group if they were captured.

 How did the Vietcong use disguise as part of its tactics?

Vietcong *(p.39)* fighters dressed as normal villagers, so US soldiers couldn't tell them apart from civilians. This led to a lot of ordinary people losing their lives.

 What were the Vietcong's tactics regarding the peasants?

The Vietcong *(p.39)* worked to get the support of the peasants in 4 key ways:

- ☑ They rarely attacked peasants or their property.
- ☑ They seized land from the wealthy and redistributed it among the poor, providing food and supplies.
- ☑ However, they were known to kill those who refused to support them. Between 1966 and 1971, 27,000 civilians were killed by the Vietcong *(p.39)*.
- ☑ They used propaganda to convince people they were beating the US Army. This included images of women and children, to show that everyone was helping to rid Vietnam of the Americans.

 What were the successes of the Vietcong's tactics?

The Vietcong's *(p.39)* tactics were successful in 2 main ways:

- ☑ The aim of the tactics was to 'get inside the heads' of American soldiers and scare them, which they did.
- ☑ As a result of their tactics, the Vietcong *(p.39)* was able to use American weapons against them. In 1964, a report stated that 90 per cent of Vietcong weapons were US weapons that had been captured in ambushes.

 What were the failures of the Vietcong's tactics?

The Vietcong's *(p.39)* tactics failed for 3 main reasons:

- ☑ Many civilians were mistaken as Vietcong *(p.39)* troops and killed.
- ☑ Not all Vietnamese people supported the actions of the Vietcong *(p.39)*, as terror and intimidation was sometimes used to gain local support.
- ☑ The guerrilla attacks alone were not enough to get rid of the Americans from Vietnam.

US TACTICS IN THE VIETNAM WAR

'One does not use napalm on villages and hamlets sheltering civilians if one is attempting to persuade these people of the rightness of one's cause'.
American comment on Vietnam

What tactics did the USA use in the Vietnam War to fight against the Vietcong?

The USA had one of the most feared armies in the world as it was well trained and well equipped. But the USA's military resources were no match for the Vietcong's *(p.39)* guerrilla warfare. The US had to alter its tactics against the Vietcong as the war progressed.

What kind of soldiers did the USA send to combat the Vietcong's tactics in Vietnam?

When the war started the USA sent experienced GIs, or general infantryman, to fight against the Vietcong *(p.39)*. However, as fatalities and casualties piled up they increasingly sent younger, less experienced troops.

What was a GI, sent by the USA to combat Vietcong tactics in Vietnam?

American soldiers in the Second World War started calling themselves GIs, which stood for 'general infantryman'. The nickname became popular during the conflict in Vietnam. GIs faced many challenges there, which hampered America's ability to defeat the Vietcong *(p.39)* and win the war.

What were the typical features of a US soldier fighting against Vietcong tactics in Vietnam?

American GIs had 10 typical features or attributes:

- ☑ By the end of the war, the average age of a GI was 19.
- ☑ Many of the soldiers were forced to fight in Vietnam as part of military conscription, known as the draft. Soldiers had to serve for a one-year period known as a 'tour of duty'.
- ☑ Unlike the Vietcong *(p.39)*, American GIs didn't travel light. They carried ration packs, ammunition, spare uniform, and as much water as they could. No matter how much water they carried, it was never enough to quench the thirst caused by the climate of the Vietnamese jungle.
- ☑ The GIs' uniforms often rotted in Vietnam's hot, damp climate.
- ☑ GIs were often overzealous and made careless mistakes when out on patrol. They were often killed by the Vietcong's *(p.39)* booby traps.
- ☑ Many GIs came from urban cities in the USA. Many had never travelled before and were ill-prepared for the environment and culture of Vietnam.
- ☑ They carried smoke grenades, to let US helicopters know when and where to extract them from the jungle.
- ☑ They carried fragmentation, or frag, grenades. When they exploded these sprayed red-hot fragments. However, many GIs were themselves accidentally killed by them, as the grenades often got caught on jungle plants.
- ☑ Unlike the Soviet AK-47 rifles used by the Vietcong *(p.39)*, the MI6 rifles carried by American GIs often jammed near water and mud, which was not ideal in Vietnamese jungle terrain.
- ☑ GIs wore boots with drainage holes to let the water out, and reinforced soles to combat the punji traps.

What methods did the USA use to combat Vietcong tactics in Vietnam?

The USA employed a number of tactics to fight against the Vietcong *(p.39)* guerrillas:

- ☑ 'Search and destroy', in which the US troops would enter Vietcong *(p.39)* territory, search out the enemy, and destroy them.
- ☑ Bombing campaigns, such as Operation Rolling Thunder.
- ☑ The use of explosive technology, such as pineapple bombs.
- ☑ The use of chemical warfare, including napalm and Agent Orange.
- ☑ The USA fought a war of attrition.
- ☑ The use of helicopters.

 What was the 'search and destroy' tactic used by the USA to fight against the Vietcong in Vietnam?

Search and destroy was a US military tactic that worked in the following ways:

- ☑ Bases were built that stretched all along the South Vietnamese coast and border, to launch 'search and destroy' missions into the jungle.
- ☑ American forces searched villages for the Vietcong *(p.39)*. When they found the enemy they burned down the entire village, which destroyed the Vietcong base and served as a warning to other villages not to harbour the guerrillas.
- ☑ This tactic soon earned the name 'zippo raids', as Zippo cigarette lighters were used to set fire to the thatched roofs of village houses.

 What was Operation Cedar Falls in the USA's fight against Vietcong tactics in Vietnam?

Operation Cedar Falls was an example of 'search and destroy'. In 1967, 750 Vietcong *(p.39)* were killed. Despite early successes, the guerrillas soon returned. The level of violence created 4 million refugees, which increased the unpopularity of the South Vietnamese and USA.

 Why was the USA's tactic of 'search and destroy' a failure fighting against Vietcong tactics in Vietnam?

The USA's tactic of 'search and destroy' failed for a number of reasons:

- ☑ US soldiers were simply not cut out to cope with the Vietcong's *(p.39)* guerrilla tactics.
- ☑ America's superior technology of heavy weapons and aircraft were better suited to open combat, but the Vietcong *(p.39)* did not engage with that method of fighting.
- ☑ As US troops searched for the enemy they were taken by surprise and attacked. The Vietcong *(p.39)* fighters would disappear back into the jungle before the Americans could respond.
- ☑ Young and inexperienced GIs could not tell the difference between Vietcong *(p.39)* soldiers and innocent villagers, and killed many ordinary civilians.

 How did the USA use Operation Rolling Thunder to fight against Vietcong tactics in Vietnam?

Operation Rolling Thunder was a major bombing campaign that lasted 3 years. It was an important US tactic.

- ☑ B-52 bombers dropped millions of tonnes of explosives.
- ☑ It targeted the Ho Chi Minh Trail and industrial targets but not Hanoi, the capital of North Vietnam. As the campaign progressed, targets also included towns and cities in South Vietnam, and Vietcong *(p.39)* bases in Laos and Cambodia.
- ☑ It cost the USA $4 billion, and killed 90,000 people.
- ☑ President Johnson wanted to bomb the Vietcong *(p.39)* into submission.

 Why did the tactics used by the USA in Operation Rolling Thunder fail against the Vietcong in Vietnam?

There were 2 main reasons the bombing tactics of Operation Rolling Thunder failed:

- ☑ Supplies continued to get through to the Vietcong *(p.39)* via the extensive tunnel system and the Ho Chi Minh Trail.

☑ Destroying industry didn't have an effect, as China and the USSR were sending military supplies to North Vietnam.

 ### How did the USA use 'pineapple bombs' to fight against Vietcong tactics in Vietnam?

The USA developed a new weapon called the 'pineapple bomb', which exploded in the air and released 500 smaller bombs that caused huge damage. It was developed to maim rather than kill, so when someone was wounded, others would help - taking their attention away from the battle.

 ### How did the USA use chemical weapons to fight against Vietcong tactics in Vietnam?

When the bombing campaigns failed to defeat the Vietcong *(p.39)*, the Americans started to use chemical weapons. The 3 most widely used were:

☑ Agent Orange, a toxic weed killer used to destroy the jungle so the Ho Chi Minh trail could be seen from the air.

☑ Agent Blue, a weed killer used to destroy crops so the Vietcong *(p.39)* would have no food.

☑ Napalm, a combustible chemical used to destroy the jungle.

 ### What tactics were used by the USA in Operation Ranch Hand to fight against the Vietcong in Vietnam?

Operation Ranch Hand saw 3,000 villages sprayed with chemicals across 24% of South Vietnam. Water supplies were poisoned. There were some fatalities and many ongoing health problems.

 ### What were the problems with the USA's use of chemical weapons to fight against Vietcong tactics in Vietnam?

The use of chemical weapons was inhumane. Agent Orange and Agent Blue led to people developing cancer and caused birth defects in newborns. Napalm burned through victims' skin, muscle and bone.

 ### What were the US Zippo raids tactics Vietnam?

US soldiers used cigarette lighters, known as Zippos, to burn down villages suspected of housing Vietcong *(p.39)* soldiers.

 ### How did the USA use attrition warfare against the Vietcong tactics in Vietnam?

The US tactic of attrition meant focusing on killing as many Vietnamese soldiers as possible. It is estimated that around 1 million North Vietnamese and Vietcong *(p.39)* soldiers died, compared to 55,000 Americans. However, this tactic did not bring success for the US.

 ### How did the USA use helicopters to fight against the Vietcong tactics in Vietnam?

Helicopters were used in 3 key ways.

☑ They were used to bring troops to a battle zone quickly, over difficult terrain.

☑ They supported ground troops during 'search and destroy' missions.

☑ They were used to evacuate wounded soldiers.

 ### What was the McNamara Line tactic used by the US in Vietnam?

The McNamara Line, named after US secretary of defence Robert McNamara, was an electronic infiltration barrier that attempted to block the Ho Chi Minh Trail with barbed wire and mines. It was eventually abandoned due to the severity of attacks on US troops.

 ### What were the successes of the USA's tactics used to fight against the Vietcong in Vietnam?

Overall, the US Army had little success. They did damage some of the supply lines along the Ho Chi Minh trail. However, the trail was so extensive it made little difference, making it impossible for the US to gain a strategic advantage in the war.

What were the failures of the USA's tactics to fight against the Vietcong in Vietnam?

Not only did US tactics result in the capture of very few Vietcong *(p.39)*, their tactics alienated ordinary people. Many innocent people were killed, and the local people turned to the Vietcong due to the tactics employed by the US forces. Their use of chemical warfare was also condemned around the world for its abuse of human rights.

DID YOU KNOW?

The M-16 rifles were unpopular with US troops and prone to jam, so it was common for soldiers to use AK-47s captured from the Vietcong instead.

THE TET OFFENSIVE 1968

'What the hell is going on? I thought we were winning this war'.
Walter Cronkite

 What happened during the Tet Offensive?

The Tet Offensive was a significant turning point in the Vietnam War. The US government had told the public it was doing well in its fight against the Vietcong *(p.39)* and would soon be able to bring the war to an end. However, just months later, the North Vietnamese and the Vietcong launched a series of major attacks in South Vietnam.

 When did the Tet Offensive start?

The Tet Offensive started on 30th January, 1968. There was supposed to a ceasefire to allow for celebrations in honour of Tet, a Vietnamese holiday celebrating the lunar new year.

Where did the Tet Offensive happen?

Hundreds of towns, cities and military bases were attacked during the Tet Offensive, along with General Westmoreland's base and the US embassy building, both in Saigon.

 What was General Westmoreland's role in the Tet Offensive?

General Westmoreland was the commander of the US Army in Vietnam. He played a key role in the Tet Offensive as the attacks caught him off guard. Months earlier he had presented the view to Congress that the war was going well. He said: 'We will prevail in Vietnam over the communist aggressor.'.

 Why did the Tet Offensive happen?

The Tet Offensive had two aims:

- ✅ The Vietcong *(p.39)* and North Vietnamese government hoped it would win them support from the South Vietnamese against the Americans, inspiring them to get rid of the current government and force the Americans from the country.
- ✅ They hoped a decisive victory against the Americans would attract media attention in the USA, weakening support from the war from its citizens.

What were the key events in the Tet Offensive?

There were a number of key events in the Tet Offensive:

- ✅ In the build up to the Tet Offensive the Vietcong *(p.39)* carried out smaller attacks, away from important cities, to draw US troops. Around 50,000 American GIs were sent to defend these areas.

- On 30th January, 84,000 Vietcong *(p.39)* and North Vietnamese soldiers launched a number of attacks across Vietnam.
- The Americans were on the back foot to begin with. However, they recovered and quickly recaptured the towns, cities and bases taken by the enemy during the attacks.
- The American embassy in Saigon was retaken by US paratroopers within hours.
- The communist forces were defeated in the Tet Offensive. 50,000 North Vietnamese troops and 10,000 Vietcong *(p.39)* soldiers were killed.

Why was the USA shocked by the Tet Offensive?

The US government and media had given Americans the impression they were winning the war. The Tet Offensive changed public opinion, as many began to see the reality.

How many casualties were there in the Tet Offensive?

Around 50,000 Vietcong *(p.39)* fighters died, compared to 2,500 American soldiers.

What were the failures of the Tet Offensive for the Vietcong?

Militarily, the Tet Offensive was a defeat for the Vietcong *(p.39)* and North Vietnam. They lost thousands of soldiers, and the USA re-took all cities, towns and bases.

What were the successes of the Tet Offensive for the Vietcong?

The Tet Offensive was both a political and psychological victory for a number of reasons.

- They had shown they could strike at any moment, and could take key cities and bases.
- The events were shown across US television, and the public saw the chaos and destruction. Americans now came to realise that, despite the clear advantage American military should have had, they were proving to be no match to the Vietcong's *(p.39)* guerrilla tactics.
- The American public started to turn against President Johnson and the USA's involvement in the Vietnam War. This was one of the Vietcong's *(p.39)* aims.

What were the results of the Tet Offensive?

The Tet Offensive was a huge turning point in the war, and had a number of consequences.

- The Americans began to question their involvement in Vietnam. They had been told, months before, that the end of the war was close. The Tet Offensive showed them that this was not true.
- The USA had spent vast sums of money, and many people had lost loved ones in the jungle of Vietnam, but the Vietcong *(p.39)* were able to strike a blow at the US embassy and showed no signs of letting up. It became clear to the US public that the war was not going to be over soon.
- In March 1968, President Johnson told the US public that he would not be running in the next presidential election.
- In June 1968, General Westmoreland was replaced by General Creighton Abrams. It was clear that Johnson was not happy with Westmoreland when he requested 200,000 more troops, and he turned down the request.
- The Tet Offensive had woken people up to the fact that the USA was now spending $30 billion a year fighting the Vietcong *(p.39)*, and 300 Americans were being killed every week in Vietnam.
- The Tet Offensive had also killed many civilians and destroyed many cities, further weakening support for the war.

What were the consequences of the Tet Offensive for the Vietcong?

The Vietcong *(p.39)* had expected the south to rise up in revolt, but this didn't happen; instead, the Vietcong was nearly wiped out. Between them, the Vietcong and the North Vietnamese Army lost around 45,000 men.

THE MY LAI MASSACRE 1968

'Something rather dark and bloody...'
US soldier Ronald Ridenhour

What was the My Lai Massacre?

American troops went to the village of My Lai to search for Vietcong *(p.39)*. The American troops killed and abused over 500 women, children and old men.

When did the My Lai Massacre happen?

The My Lai Massacre happened on 16th March, 1968, not long after the Tet Offensive *(p.52)* began.

Where did the My Lai Massacre happen?

The massacre happened in a village called My Lai, in the Quang Ngai region of South Vietnam.

Who was involved in the My Lai Massacre?

Approximately 80 US soldiers from Charlie Company, a unit of the army's 11th Infantry Brigade, took part in the massacre.

Why did the My Lai Massacre happen?

There were 2 key reasons the massacre happened:

- ✅ Charlie Company was sent on a search and destroy *(p.50)* mission, following reports of a base of 200 Vietcong *(p.39)* fighters in the area of My Lai. Reports suggested locals were giving them food, shelter and weapons, so Charlie Company was sent to burn all crops, livestock and food.

- ✅ Charlie Company had lost 5 soldiers in the Tet Offensive *(p.52)*. Although the unit had never directly fought the Vietcong *(p.39)*, it had experienced the organisation's guerrilla warfare while on patrol. It is thought the war had taken a psychological toll on the soldiers.

What were the key events in the My Lai Massacre?

There were a number of key events in the My Lai Massacre:

- ✅ At 7:30am on 16th March, 1968, 9 American helicopters landed near the village of My Lai. It was a Saturday, and it was expected all the villagers would be at the market.

- ✅ Upon landing, the soldiers started shooting at any house they thought might contain Vietcong *(p.39)* soldiers.

- ✅ Grenades were used to destroy houses, crops and livestock.

- ✅ Some villagers tried to escape but the US forces shot or stabbed them. This was completely unwarranted; none of the villagers had retaliated and most of those present were women and children.

- ✅ There were also several reports of Charlie Company troops torturing and raping civilians.

- ✅ No Vietcong *(p.39)* soldiers were found, and only a few weapons were recovered.

Charlie Company returned to base and said 22 civilians were killed by accident, and the remaining dead were Vietcong *(p.39)*.

How was the My Lai Massacre covered up?

At first, Charlie Company received much recognition for its efforts. As the truth emerged, the government attempted a cover up:

 The government announced the troops had killed 128 Vietcong *(p.39)* fighters and destroyed their base.

 However, some soldiers and local inhabitants reported what had really happened.

 The army attempted a cover-up, but one soldier, Ronald Ridenhour, made his eye-witness account public. He wrote more than 30 letters to politicians and military officials, saying 'something rather dark and bloody' had happened in My Lai a year earlier.

 General Westmoreland received one of Ridenhour's letters. Although he didn't believe it, he ordered an inquiry. The army later admitted to 20 accidental civilian deaths.

What happened when the My Lai Massacre was investigated?

Two inquiries were held into the events of the My Lai Massacre, one by the government and the other by the army.

What did the government's investigation conclude about the My Lai Massacre?

The government investigation into the My Lai Massacre came to two main conclusions:

 It interviewed 398 witnesses and the weight of evidence indicated Charlie Company had massacred approximately 347 unarmed civilians.

 All those involved in the torture, rape, murder and cover up of the massacre should be punished.

What did the army's investigation into the My Lai Massacre conclude?

The army's investigation reported widespread failures and came to several conclusions:

 There were significant failures in the leadership and discipline of the soldiers.

 The soldiers were not experienced enough to carry out the roles they had been assigned to.

 The psychological trauma experienced by the men of Charlie Company created a desire for revenge against the Vietnamese.

 25 men should be prosecuted for the massacre, either because of their participation or their involvement in the cover up.

How many were prosecuted because of their role in the My Lai Massacre?

Although the army said 25 men should be prosecuted, and some did face murder charges, only Lieutenant William Calley was prosecuted.

Who was Lieutenant Calley in the My Lai Massacre?

Lieutenant William Calley was one of the soldiers in charge of Charlie Company on the day of the massacre. He was responsible for the murder of 109 civilians at My Lai.

What was the role of Lieutenant Calley in the My Lai Massacre?

Calley played a leading role in the day's events. In accounts of what happened from other soldiers, Calley is reported to have said the following:

 In response to questions about a group of men, women and children gathered in the centre of the village by soldiers, he said: 'You know what I want you to do with them.'.

 On returning 10 minutes later and finding the group still there, he said: 'Haven't you got rid of them yet? I want them dead. Waste them.'.

What happened to Lieutenant Calley following his trial for the My Lai Massacre?

Lieutenant Calley was sentenced to life imprisonment. President Nixon received more than 5,000 telegrams in protest as many were outraged by the sentence, believing Calley was only following orders. In response, Calley was confined to an army base on President Nixon's orders and released after three and a half years.

 What was the public's response to the My Lai Massacre?

Newspaper reports surfaced in November 1970 that claimed more than 500 civilians had been murdered in the massacre. On 5th December, pictures taken by an army photographer were shown on television, prompting a massive outcry.

 What were the consequences of the My Lai Massacre?

The My Lai Massacre had 3 main consequences:

- ☑ It greatly strengthened the growing peace movement. People were repulsed by the atrocities committed by Charlie Company and questioned the morality of the USA's involvement in Vietnam.

- ☑ Due to the cover up of the massacre, people distrusted the government and the army. They did not believe they were being told the full truth about the war.

- ☑ The massacre led to further investigations and, in 1971, it was found over a third of US troops were addicted to drugs. It was clear morale was at an all-time low.

DID YOU KNOW?

The My Lai Massacre was initially known as the Pinkville Massacre, after the slang name used by US troops for the area.

THE DRAFT SYSTEM

'I ain't got no quarrel with those Vietcong'.
Muhammad Ali 1967

 What was the draft system for the Vietnam War?

Any man aged over 18 could be drafted into compulsory military service. Most were under 26, and the average was 19 years of age.

 What training did people who were drafted into the Vietnam War receive?

Draftees received only basic training before being sent to fight in Vietnam.

 What was the response to the draft system in the Vietnam War?

Many people felt the draft was unfair, that the draftees were too young, and that a lack of proper training increased the chances of them dying.

 What was the lottery system of the draft in the Vietnam War?

In 1969, to try and make the system fairer, the government turned the draft into a random lottery system. Men aged from 25 to 31 were included, adding a further 26 million potential soldiers. Out of 2.6 million men who fought in Vietnam, 650,000 were draftees.

Was anyone exempt from the draft in the Vietnam War?

4 main groups were exempt from the draft:

☑ The physically and mentally unfit.

☑ University students.

☑ Some government and industrial workers.

☑ Only sons, or those who could prove being drafted would create hardship for their families.

 How many men were made exempt from the draft in the Vietnam War?

In total, 15 million men were made exempt from the draft.

 What were the views of conscientious objectors on the draft for the Vietnam War?

Men could become conscientious objectors (COs) and refuse military service on the grounds of their religious or moral beliefs.

 What work did conscientious objectors do as part of the draft system in the Vietnam War?

Conscientious objectors were required to undertake war work, such as working in weapons factories. There were around 17,000 COs in total, although almost 20 times as many men applied for exemption.

 How did people avoid the draft in the Vietnam War?

Men living or working abroad could avoid the draft, but this option was only really available to the wealthy. Some 50,000 men went into hiding or left America illegally instead.

 Why was the draft system unfair in the Vietnam War?

There were 3 main reasons the draft system was seen as unfair:

☑ Middle-class white men were often able to avoid the draft as they could afford to go to university or move abroad.

☑ Those with influential contacts could also dodge the draft.

☑ A disproportionate number of poor people, and those belonging to black and ethnic minorities, were therefore called up.

 How many people refused to obey the draft for the Vietnam War?

9,000 men were prosecuted for refusing to be drafted.

 What was the significance of the draft system in the Vietnam War?

The significance of the draft system to the Vietnam War was its impact on the growing peace movement. Many people saw the system as unfair and engaged in protests.

DID YOU KNOW?

Heavyweight boxer Muhammad Ali was stripped of his boxing licence and sentenced to five years in prison as a result of his stance as a conscientious objector.

OPPOSITION TO THE VIETNAM WAR

'Hey, Hey LBJ; How many kids did you kill today?'
Anti-war folk song and chant

 ## Who opposed the war in Vietnam?

As the Vietnam War progressed, anti-war sentiment and protests increased, peaking between 1968 and 1970. 700,000 protested against the war in Washington DC, in November 1969.

 ## Why was there opposition to the Vietnam War?

Opposition to the Vietnam War was based around 4 key arguments.

- ☑ Many people objected to the expense of the war, and felt that the money would be better spent on the USA's domestic problems.
- ☑ Civil rights activists felt that many aspects of the war, including the draft system *(p.56)*, reflected the racism in American society and placed black people disproportionately at risk.
- ☑ The USA was not winning the war, and the casualties were high. Many Americans felt that the human cost was too high.
- ☑ An increasing number of people believed that the USA's stance in Vietnam was unethical.

 ## Who led the opposition to the Vietnam War?

The protest movement against the Vietnam War was led by civil rights activists and the student movement.

 ## Why did people oppose the expense of the Vietnam War?

There were 3 main reasons why people opposed the cost of the Vietnam War:

- ☑ Overall, the cost of the Vietnam War was $167 billion.
- ☑ Many Americans lived in poverty. Those who opposed the Vietnam War felt that the US should solve its own social problems before interfering, and spending money on a country thousands of miles away.
- ☑ Many Americans believed that the Vietnam War was a result of the 'military-industrial complex', a group of businessmen and military leaders who would benefit from the conflict. President Eisenhower had warned against these groups in 1961.

 ## Why did civil rights activists oppose the Vietnam War?

Civil rights activists pointed out 3 key issues of inequality and racism that were highlighted by the Vietnam War:

- ☑ African Americans were more likely to be have to go to war - 30% were drafted, compared to 19% of white Americans.
- ☑ African Americans were also more likely to be wounded in the fighting. 11% of US troops were black, and yet they made up 22% of the casualties.
- ☑ Some African Americans pointed out that they were expected to fight on behalf of a country that treated them unfairly and with prejudice.

 ## Why did people oppose the human cost of the Vietnam War?

Many anti-war protesters were concerned about the human cost of the war in Vietnam, and the effect of young American men who were forced to fight.

- ☑ Over 58,000 US soldiers were killed in the fighting.
- ☑ Over 303,000 US soldiers were wounded.
- ☑ Many more returned home traumatised by their experiences. The suicide rate amongst men who had fought in Vietnam was twice that of those who had not.

Quizzes, amazing exam preparation tools and more at GCSEHistory.com

☑ The average age of a US soldier was just nineteen, and many had never been in the military before. People felt that the war represented a loss of their innocence.

☑ These views were reinforced when veterans returned home and condemned what they had experienced.

 Why did people oppose the Vietnam War as unethical?

Over the course of the Vietnam War, people increasingly began to feel that the Vietnam War was wrong for 5 key reasons.

☑ The USA's role in failing to support democratic elections in South Vietnam and the Geneva Accords suggested that it was not really concerned with upholding the principles of democracy and choice.

☑ Television and newspaper reports showed shocking scenes of devastation and suffering, involving civilians and children.

☑ The Tet Offensive *(p.52)* in 1968 involved the killing of many civilians as the USA fought back. It also demonstrated that the USA was not even winning the war.

☑ The killing of civilians in the My Lai Massacre *(p.54)* in 1968 horrified Americans when it was reported a year later.

☑ The use of US troops and bombing in Cambodia and Laos in 1970-71 increased these concerns.

 Why did politicians oppose the Vietnam War?

As opposition to the war grew, the attitudes of politicians reflected the changing attitudes of their electorate. Congress revoked the Gulf of Tonkin Resolution *(p.45)*, and set a deadline of December 1971 for the total withdrawal of US troops from Vietnam.

 How did students oppose the Vietnam War?

Student groups often led the protests against the Vietnam War in 3 main ways.

☑ In the first half of 1968, 40,000 students were involved in protests.

☑ Student protesters attracted a lot of media attention because they were often young, white and middle-class.

☑ Four students were killed in 1970 when national guardsmen shot at protesters at Kent State University.

DID YOU KNOW?

Songs written in protest of the Vietnam War include Bob Dylan's 'Blowin' in the Wind', Nina Simone's 'Backlash Blues' and John Lennon's 'Give Peace A Chance'.

THE IMPACT OF THE MEDIA

'The only rational way out then will be to negotiate, not as victors, but as an honorable people who lived up to their pledge to defend democracy, and did the best they could.'

 What media coverage was there of the Vietnam War?

US media coverage continued to expand as the war continued. In 1964 there were fewer than 10 journalists in Vietnam, but by 1968 there were over 600. Television also played a part in bringing the war into American homes.

 What are some examples of media coverage of the Vietnam War?

Examples of media coverage of the Vietnam War included:

☑ The Tet Offensive *(p.52)* in January 1968. Coverage showed Vietnamese civilians being killed and ancient monuments destroyed.

✅ In February 1968 there were news stories of General Nguyen Ngoc Loan's execution of a Vietcong *(p.39)* fighter.

✅ In November 1969 the media broke the truth about the My Lai Massacre *(p.54)*.

 ## Why was there an increase in media coverage of the Vietnam War?

Media coverage of the Vietnam War increased for the following reasons:

✅ To begin with, there were few troops in Vietnam. In 1960 there were only 900 'military advisers', and no reporters.

✅ This changed in 1960 when local Vietnamese people were killed in an attack against Diem *(p.37)*, the South Vietnamese president. Many journalists travelled to Vietnam to report on the event.

✅ As US involvement in the war increased, so too did the number of journalists covering the conflict. By 1965 there were 400 foreign news reporters in Vietnam - an increase of 900 per cent on 1964.

✅ Since the Second World War, there had been a significant increase in the number of Americans who owned a television. In 1948, just 1 per cent of American households had a television; by 1961, this had risen to 93 per cent.

✅ Journalists were better equipped to report the news with ground-breaking technology such as video cameras and voice recorders. It helped reporters capture the reality of the war and broadcast it to America and the world.

✅ There was no censorship on coverage of the Vietnam War. The Second World War and Korean War *(p.16)* had been filmed by military cameramen, but Vietnam was caught on film by by independent television networks.

 ## What was the early media coverage of the Vietnam War like?

Early coverage of events in Vietnam mostly included positive reporting on the courage of American soldiers and the new technology used in weaponry. In the context of the Cold War, it portrayed the USA as the 'goodies', fighting the communist 'baddies' of North Vietnam.

 ## How was the anti-Vietnam War movement portrayed on television?

The media showed the anti-war movement and created momentum for it through television, music, and key public figures.

 ## How did television portray the civil rights movement's views on the Vietnam War?

Civil rights activists such as Martin Luther King, Muhammad Ali, and the Black Panthers were among those who spoke out. They opposed black people having to fight for America when they faced racism at home.

 ## How was music used in coverage of the anti-Vietnam War movement on television?

Music was a massive medium for the anti-war movement to express its beliefs. Music from Bob Dylan, John Lennon and Jimi Hendrix among others helped create a young generation that opposed the war.

 ## What were the 'five o'clock follies' in media coverage of the Vietnam War?

As the war intensified in the mid 1960s, US forces met with journalists covering the conflict daily at 5:00pm. The journalists would jeer and mock the military officials as they felt the truth was being hidden about the extent of failures of the US Army in Vietnam. These meetings became known as the 'five o'clock follies' as they were seen as useless.

 ## What was the significance of media coverage of the Tet Offensive in the Vietnam War?

The TV media coverage of the Tet Offensive *(p.52)* was significant for the following reasons:

✅ The coverage resulted in a change in how the war was reported and how the public perceived the conflict.

✅ For many months officials had assured the public that they were winning the war, however the TV media coverage of the Tet Offensive *(p.52)* contradicted this.

✅ TV reports of the Tet Offensive *(p.52)* showed the fall of the US embassy of Saigon - a symbolic defeat in the eyes of Americans (although the US eventually won it back).

✅ Viewers saw the brutality of the war, and after the Tet Offensive *(p.52)* many people did not trust what they were being told.

How did media coverage expose the government's lies to the public about the Vietnam War?

People lost faith when they realised the government was not being completely honest about what was happening in Vietnam. For example, the US government claimed victory in the Tet Offensive *(p.52)*, but CBS journalist Walter Cronkite reported the reality and showed that it was a stalemate.

What was the 'credibility gap' on television during the Vietnam War?

The 'credibility gap' was the term used to describe the difference between what the US government said was happening, and what people saw happening on TV.

What was the significance of Walter Cronkite's role in media coverage of the Vietnam War?

The role of Walter Cronkite was significant for the following reasons:

- ☑ Walter Cronkite was a famous news broadcaster, seen as one of the 'most trusted men in America'. His coverage of the war played a huge role in the peace movement.

- ☑ In one of his news broadcasts for CBS, in February 1967, he said: 'It seems now more certain than ever, that the bloody experience of Vietnam is to end a stalemate... it is increasingly clear to the only rational way out then will be to negotiate.'.

- ☑ Cronkite was so influential that President Johnson once said to an advisor: 'If I have lost Cronkite, I've lost this country.'.

- ☑ When Walter Cronkite made his famous statement on the Tet Offensive *(p.52)* in 1968, it was considered a turning point in the media and public attitude, and the beginning of the fading of support for the war.

What was the significance of media coverage of the My Lai Massacre in the Vietnam War?

Coverage of the My Lai Massacre *(p.54)* in March 1968, was significant because it damaged the reputation of the US forces. Americans were shocked and appalled about both the reports of their soldiers murdering innocent people but also the fact that the army and government had tried to cover it up.

What was the impact of media coverage of the Vietnam War?

The TV media coverage of the Vietnam War had the following impacts:

- ☑ It led to a lack of trust in the US Army and the government. When the New York Times published leaked reports of American actions in Vietnam in June 1971 that were supposed to be secret many felt they had been lied to about the war.

- ☑ The media coverage influenced public opinion. When the names and faces of over 200 US soldiers were published during a week of fighting in 1969, people became angry about fighting a distant war.

- ☑ As more and more stories were published of soldiers and civilians dying and the brutality of the war, this affected the morale and behaviour in the US forces.

- ☑ The failure of US tactics in Vietnam was widely published and clear for Americans to see on the television and this led to more people questioning the point of the war and if the USA could win.

- ☑ The anti-war movement was further strengthened by the TV media coverage of the conflict.

DID YOU KNOW?

Walter Cronkite broke the news of the assassinations of John F Kennedy, Martin Luther King and John Lennon.

THE NIXON DOCTRINE

*'I would rather be a one-term President and do what I believe is right than to be a two-term President
at the cost of seeing America become a second-rate power'.*
Richard Nixon, 1970

 What was the Nixon Doctrine?

The Nixon Doctrine set out the US government's foreign policy on how it would support allies who faced military threats. The US would supply them with money and equipment, but no troops. This became known as Vietnamisation *(p.62)*.

 When was the Nixon Doctrine introduced?

The Nixon Doctrine was introduced on 25th July, 1969.

 Who was responsible for the Nixon Doctrine?

President Richard Nixon was elected in 1969, and changed the US approach to the Vietnam War. This approach was outlined in the Nixon Doctrine.

 What happened because of the Nixon Doctrine?

The Nixon Doctrine created the policy known as Vietnamisation *(p.62)*.

 What did Nixon say in the Nixon Doctrine?

In a speech in July 1969, Nixon said that America would honour any treaties it had already made, and would support its allies against any threat by providing training for their troops. However, no US troops would be sent to help.

What did Vietnamisation mean under the Nixon Doctrine?

Vietnamisation *(p.62)* was another name given to Nixon's approach. It meant the USA could 'withdraw with honour', and would allow South Vietnam to remain an independent, non-communist country.

How was the reaction to the Nixon Doctrine divided?

The South Vietnamese government felt that the US was withdrawing before the ARVN was ready to take over. However, the American people wanted the Vietnamisation *(p.62)* that Nixon had promised.

DID YOU KNOW?

Richard Nixon is the only US president to resign from office, after the Watergate Scandal.

VIETNAMISATION

'After 5 years of Americans going into Vietnam, we are finally bringing American men home'.
Richard Nixon, 1969

 What was Vietnamisation?

Vietnamisation was a US policy to end American involvement in Vietnam by developing the South Vietnamese army.

Quizzes, amazing exam preparation tools and more at GCSEHistory.com

When was the policy of Vietnamisation introduced?

The policy of Vietnamisation was officially announced on 3rd November, 1969. By spring 1972, when US forces attacked Laos, it was evident the policy was failing.

 Who was involved in the policy of Vietnamisation?

The policy of Vietnamisation was the idea of President Nixon, who implemented it during his time in office.

 What were the aims of the policy of Vietnamisation?

The policy of Vietnamisation had a number of aims:

☑ It aimed to make the ARVN self-sufficient, so it could defend South Vietnam without US support.

☑ This, in turn, would enable Nixon to withdraw US troops from Vietnam.

 Why was the policy of Vietnamisation introduced?

The policy of Vietnamisation was introduced for a number of reasons:

☑ Nixon was realistic about the unlikelihood of victory in Vietnam, and knew he had to bring an end to the war.

☑ Nixon could not use nuclear weapons to do this, so he had to find another way.

☑ Nixon was anti-communist and did not want South Vietnam to fall to communism.

☑ Nixon believed the South Vietnamese should take responsibility for their own defence.

☑ Nixon needed to find a practical solution to the war quickly, as a poll in early 1969 showed 56 per cent of Americans thought US involvement in Vietnam was wrong.

 What problems did President Nixon face when implementing the policy of Vietnamisation?

At the same time as Nixon implemented Vietnamisation, with the intention of withdrawing US troops, he was also extending the war into into Cambodia and Laos. For this, he needed more soldiers. In April 1970 he announced 100,000 more troops were needed, prompting widespread demonstrations across the USA.

 How did the policy of Vietnamisation work?

There were a number of aspects to the policy of Vietnamisation:

☑ The USA was to provide training and equipment for the expansion of the ARVN.

☑ Local villagers would be recruited as civilian militia, in charge of securing rural areas.

☑ The ARVN would take a more direct role in seeking out the Vietcong (p.39). Since 1965 they had taken a back seat to the US.

☑ Between 1968 and 1971, the ARVN was increased from 393,000 to 532,000 troops.

☑ As the ARVN became more self-sufficient, US troops would be withdrawn from Vietnam. The first notable departure was on 7th July, 1969.

☑ By the beginning of 1970 the ARNV had been equipped with $4 billion worth of military supplies, including rifles, artillery, munitions, and helicopters.

☑ ARNV officers had received specialised training in command, military strategy, and counter-insurgency warfare.

 What were the official peace talks during Vietnamisation?

Nixon began the long and difficult process of sending representatives to negotiate with both North and South Vietnam, as well as the Vietcong (p.39).

 What were the secret peace talks during Vietnamisation?

Nixon held secret peace talks with North Vietnam's leader, Le Duc Tho, sending Henry Kissinger to negotiate.

How many US troops were withdrawn during Vietnamisation?

President Nixon said he was decreasing the number of US troops in Vietnam by 25,000. The withdrawal started in July 1969.

 ### Why did they train the ARVN during Vietnamisation?

General Abrams was ordered to focus on training the ARVN so it could continue the war without the support of US troops.

 ### What were the secret bombings ordered by Nixon during Vietnamisation?

In March 1969, President Nixon ordered bombs to be dropped on the Ho Chi Minh Trail in Cambodia. He did this due to the presence of Vietnamese communists and because it was also being used as a supply trail. He wanted to pressure the North Vietnamese into negotiating.

 ### Was the policy of Vietnamisation successful?

The policy of Vietnamisation made South Vietnam one of the most militarised countries in Asia, and half the South Vietnamese population had been recruited. But it was a failure.

 ### How did the harvest cause Vietnamisation to fail?

In 1972, a poor harvest led to economic hardship. Little or no support was given to the South Vietnamese people.

 ### How did corruption cause Vietnamisation to fail?

The stealing of supplies and equipment was common. Officers regularly took bribes, which allowed thieves to steal goods. This cost the US Army millions of dollars in lost equipment, and meant that troops were not adequately supplied. This made winning the war harder.

 ### How did funding cause the failure of Vietnamisation?

The amount of funding available was restricted by the US Congress. This limited the capability and options available to the US military.

 ### How did the inadequate training of the ARVN troops lead to the failure of the policy of Vietnamisation?

The training of ARVN troops was rushed. Instructions for equipment use and operation were given in English, which the Vietnamese could not understand. Without US support, the ARVN was unable to continue fighting.

 ### How did the unpopularity of the South Vietnamese government lead to the failure of the policy of Vietnamisation?

The South Vietnamese people disliked their own government. It was weak and divided, and they saw it as a puppet of a US administration that was also corrupt. It could not survive without billions of dollars of aid provided by America.

 ### How did the military weaknesses and the corruption of the ARNV lead to the failure of the policy of Vietnamisation?

American had thrown significant funding at the ARVN, but they couldn't change the fact it was a much divided organisation, riddled with corruption and incompetence. Even though the US had provided training, its leaders were incapable of commanding the respect of their men, and did not have the morale needed to combat the Vietcong (p. 39).

How did the economic weaknesses of South Vietnam lead to the failure of the policy of Vietnamisation?

The USA had been propping up the South Vietnamese government since the 1950s, and it had become dependent on American funding. At the same time, the US was looking to gradually withdraw funding, while the USSR and China were sending significant funds to the government in North Vietnam.

PEACE NEGOTIATIONS

'We wrested total victory,'
Le Duc Tho, 1985'

 What was the role of peace negotiations at the end of the Vietnam War?

These were the discussions that took place before the Paris Peace Accords that ended the Vietnam War.

 What was the background to the peace negotiations for the end of the Vietnam War?

President Nixon promised to end the war in his election campaign of 1968. He started talks with China and the USSR to try to end the Vietnam War. North Vietnam worried they wouldn't be able to continue fighting without their allies, so in 1970 they agreed to talks with the US.

 What were America's demands in the negotiations to end the Vietnam War?

President Johnson had mentioned, as early as April 1965, that the USA would negotiate at any time, but that an independent South Vietnam must be guaranteed.

 What were the North Vietnamese demands in the negotiations for the end of the war in Vietnam?

They wanted a united Vietnam to be part of any peace talks, and they expected a communist government to be elected.

 What happened when talks began between the USA and North Vietnam for the war to end?

Following the 1968 Tet Offensive *(p.52)*, both sides decided to hold talks in Paris, but they simply stated their previous positions.

 Why was the USA under pressure to negotiate the end of the war in Vietnam?

There were 2 important reasons why the USA was under pressure to end the war in Vietnam.

- ☑ Opposition to the war was increasing.
- ☑ Congress had cut funding.

 What happened during the negotiations for end of the Vietnam War?

There were 3 main steps to the negotiations.

- ☑ On 8th October 1972, the USA and North Vietnam reached an agreement.
- ☑ President Thieu of South Vietnam refused to sign, because he had been left out of the talks in Paris.
- ☑ North Vietnam accused the USA of using Thieu's refusal as an excuse to back out of the agreement.

 What were the consequences of the negotiations for the end of the Vietnam War?

There were 4 important consequences to the negotiations to end the Vietnam War.

- ☑ The talks broke off.

✅ Nixon promised President Thieu weapons, supplies and aid, if he would attend the talks.

✅ Nixon asked China and the USSR to persuade the North to return to the talks.

✅ Talks resumed on 8th January, 1973.

THE PARIS ACCORDS, 1973

*'Now that we have achieved an honorable agreement, let us be proud that America did not settle for
a peace that would have betrayed our allies'.*
Richard Nixon, 1973

What were the Paris Peace Accords?

The Paris Peace Accords were agreements to end the war and restore peace in Vietnam.

When were the Paris Peace Accords signed?

They were signed on 27th January, 1973.

Who were the key figures that negotiated the Paris Peace Accords?

The key figures involved in public and secret meetings where a peace agreement was negotiated were the USA's Henry Kissinger and North Vietnam's Le Duc Tho.

Who signed the Paris Peace Accords?

There were 4 signatories to the Paris Accords:

✅ The USA.

✅ North Vietnam.

✅ South Vietnam.

✅ The National Liberation Front, otherwise known as the Vietcong *(p.39)*.

What were the agreements of the Paris Accords?

There were 7 agreements in the Paris Peace Accords:

✅ Acceptance of the reunification of Vietnam, and agreement a new government would be elected under international supervision.

✅ All four parties agreed to a ceasefire.

✅ Agreement to keep the armies of both Vietnamese governments, but the USA would not send aid to the ARVN.

✅ The USA would withdraw all troops, equipment and advisers within 60 days.

✅ All sides would exchange prisoners of war and equipment within 60 days.

✅ The USA would send aid for reconstruction to both sides.

✅ The USA government would not interfere in Vietnam in any way.

Quizzes, amazing exam preparation tools and more at GCSEHistory.com

Was peace achieved with the Paris Accords?

The Paris Peace Accords did not bring instant peace.

DID YOU KNOW?

In October 1972, Henry Kissinger worked out a peace agreement, but South Vietnam refused to sign in the fear that the US would abandon them.

THE FALL OF SAIGON 1975

'The military situation in the area deteriorated rapidly. I therefore ordered the evacuation of all American personnel remaining in South Vietnam.'
President Gerald Ford, 1975

 What was the fall of Saigon?

This was the capture of Saigon, the capital of South Vietnam, by the People's Army of Vietnam and the Vietcong *(p.39)*.

 When was the fall of Saigon?

The fall of Saigon happened on 30th April, 1975.

 What happened to US soldiers during the fall of Saigon?

The remaining US soldiers, and some Vietnamese refugees, were evacuated by helicopter.

 What was the importance of the fall of Saigon?

The fall of Saigon was important for 2 reasons:

☑ It marked the end of the Vietnam War.

☑ Vietnam became a united communist country.

DID YOU KNOW?

Saigon was renamed Ho Chi Minh City.

REASONS FOR THE USA'S FAILURE

'Television brought the brutality of war into the comfort of the living room. Vietnam was lost in the living rooms of America -- not on the battlefields of Vietnam'.
Montreal Gazette, 1975

 What caused the USA to fail in Vietnam?

The American government and public lacked a clear understanding of, or the motivation and adaptability to succeed, in Vietnam. They were also at a disadvantage culturally, politically and militarily, as they were not Vietnamese.

What were the main reasons the USA failed in Vietnam?

The 4 main reasons that contributed to the USA's failure in Vietnam were:

- ☑ The tactics and resolve of the Vietcong *(p.39)*.
- ☑ The cultural weaknesses of the USA in Vietnam.
- ☑ The political and public opposition to the war in the USA.
- ☑ The military weaknesses of the American forces.

 Why did cultural weaknesses lead to the USA failing in Vietnam?

Cultural weakness was a key reason of the USA's failure in Vietnam due to the following:

- ☑ Many Americans had racist attitudes towards the Vietnamese, meaning they did not always treat local civilians well. This led to atrocities like the My Lai Massacre *(p.54)*. US forces needed the support of the locals, but mostly alienated them.
- ☑ It was hard to gain support from the locals because they didn't speak their language and needed interpreters.
- ☑ Most Americans had no idea what the country was like. They didn't understand why villagers were unwilling to leave the lands where their ancestors were buried. This led to feelings of hatred from the local population and increased support for the Vietcong *(p.39)*.
- ☑ The Americans didn't realise most Vietnamese villagers were unable to read, so dropping leaflets warning them to leave before bombing raids happened didn't work. Millions of innocent civilians were killed during the conflict.
- ☑ Many South Vietnamese saw the USA as occupiers imposing their ideas - just as the French and Japanese had - and not advocates for democracy. They helped the Vietcong *(p.39)*, creating further difficulties for the US forces.

 Why did political and public opposition lead to the USA's failure in Vietnam?

Political and public opposition led to the USA's failure in the Vietnam War for the following reasons:

- ☑ The USA backed the South Vietnamese government, which was corrupt. Many officials had worked for the French, making America even more unpopular. Political figures and the American public objected to the USA fighting a war that defended a corrupt regime.
- ☑ The USA faced opposition at home in the form of anti-war protests, and restricted funding from Congress after 1971. This placed President Nixon under huge pressure to withdraw from Vietnam.
- ☑ The US public questioned the legitimacy of the war, meaning the US government no longer had a mandate to fight.
- ☑ Americans were horrified by media coverage of the war, and this led to a growth in the anti-war movement. By 1971, many surveys showed the majority of American people wanted US troops brought home immediately and an end to the conflict. The US government could not fight a war its people did not want.

 Why did weaknesses in the USA's military lead to its failure in Vietnam?

Military weaknesses in the US forces led to failure in Vietnam for the following reasons:

- ☑ The military believed the war could be won with more troops and through bombing campaigns in North Vietnam, which was not the limited war the government wanted. US forces also failed to adjust their tactics to suit Vietnam's terrain and climate.
- ☑ US tactics alienated locals and caused resentment. 'Search and destroy *(p.50)*' included soldiers burning the homes of villagers.
- ☑ As the war progressed more soldiers were needed, so the draft became increasingly important. It meant many young and inexperienced soldiers were posted to Vietnam - and, as they returned home after a year, they left just as they were learning how to fight in the country's tough conditions. This contributed to the high number of casualties.
- ☑ Soldiers lacked training in how to combat guerrilla tactics. Their weapon and methods were ineffective in the jungle. One key problem faced by inexperienced GIs was the inability to recognise the enemy, leading to the deaths of innocent civilians and demoralised troops.
- ☑ Discipline among US soldiers was inadequate. Drug taking and desertion - where a soldier would leave his post - were rife. Approximately 30 per cent of US troops in Vietnam used heroin, further impacting their competency to fight effectively.

Quizzes, amazing exam preparation tools and more at GCSEHistory.com

- The US military did not adapt their approach to combat the Vietcong's *(p.39)* guerrilla tactics, and therefore could not beat it.
- Their tactics often killed innocent civilians and sometimes their own troops. This led to low morale among the US forces which made it difficult for them to fight.
- With 12,000km between the USA and Vietnam, it meant US forces often had problems with their equipment and weapons.
- Racial inequalities in the US Army led to low morale and significant opposition back home. By 1970, black Americans made up 11 per cent of soldiers in Vietnam but almost 25 per cent of the casualties. Black soldiers questioned why they were fighting a war in the name of a freedom they did not have themselves.

 ### How did the strengths of the Vietcong lead to the USA's failure in Vietnam?

The strength of both the Vietcong's *(p.39)* tactics and its resolve led to US failure in Vietnam for the following reasons:

- They knew the landscape, culture and language of the south, and so could easily navigate their way around undetected. They could also garner the support of the locals.
- The Vietnamese had a history of fighting foreign invaders, namely France and Japan. They were determined to remove all foreign influences from their country.
- The Vietcong *(p.39)* was already well established in the south, so North Vietnam could work with them and send supplies using the Ho Chi Minh Trail. Many North Vietnamese fighters were originally from the south, before the 1954 Geneva Accords, and so had family and contacts they could use.
- They had international support. Between 1954 and 1967, China and the USSR sent $3 billion in aid, weapons, and equipment. Laos and Cambodia allowed the Ho Chi Minh Trail to run through their countries, and there was little America could do to stop this without further conflict.
- The North Vietnamese and Vietcong *(p.39)* troops were used to jungle conditions. They used guerrilla tactics and fought small skirmishes, although they could also fight large battles. These tactics were perfect for the terrain, and the USA could not fight effectively.
- The Vietcong *(p.39)* used a system of tunnels and bases to move supplies, troops and equipment. They were well-organised and experienced. The USA continuously failed at destroying the Vietcong's supply lines.
- The North Vietnamese and Vietcong *(p.39)* troops were fighting for their country. They had a clear motive to achieve victory and fought with fierce determination. The US troops, however, were fighting 12,000km from home for a cause they increasingly cared less about.

DID YOU KNOW?

An estimated 11% of US troops suffered from PTSD as a result of the conflict.

HOW SUCCESSFUL WAS THE POLICY OF CONTAINMENT IN VIETNAM?

'A wound to the spirit so sore that news of peace stirred only the relief that comes with an end to pain'.
Newsweek, February 1973

 ### How successful was the policy of containment in Vietnam?

Historians debate whether containment *(p.70)* was successful in Vietnam.

 ### How was US policy in Vietnam successful in achieving containment in Vietnam ?

Historians argue there are three main ways containment *(p.70)* could be seen as successful in Vietnam.

Vietnamisation *(p.62)* meant the US passed on the responsibility for defeating communism, rather than 'surrendering' - they continued to give supplies to the South Vietnamese government.

✅ The Nixon Doctrine *(p.62)*, and the move away from containment *(p.70)*, saved countless American lives.

✅ Nixon argued that he had achieved 'Peace with Honour'.

How was US policy on containment in Vietnam a failure?

Historians argue there are four main ways containment *(p.70)* could be seen as a failure in Vietnam.

✅ Vietnam remained a communist country.

✅ Vietnamisation *(p.62)* was a failure.

✅ American actions actually encouraged support for communism in Laos and Cambodia.

✅ The fall of Saigon *(p.67)* was a victory for communism.

DID YOU KNOW?

Laos and Cambodia became communist in 1975.

HOW EFFECTIVELY DID THE USA CONTAIN THE SPREAD OF COMMUNISM?

'...let us be proud that America did not settle for a peace that would have betrayed our allies...'
Richard Nixon, 1973

How effectively did the USA contain the spread of communism?

Historians debate how far the USA was able to successfully contain communism.

How was the USA successful at containing communism?

There are 6 main ways the USA was able to contain communism successfully:

✅ South Korea remained free from communism.

✅ The creation of SEATO made the growth of communism in Asia less likely.

✅ Communism would have spread further in Asia if the USA hadn't intervened. For example, Japan, Formosa, Thailand, Burma and Malaysia didn't fall to communism.

✅ Cuba no longer posed a significant military threat as Kennedy prevented nuclear missiles being placed there.

✅ Early attempts at trying to spread communism into Central and South America failed.

✅ Marshall Aid and the Truman Doctrine prevented communism from spreading further in Europe, for example with Greece in 1947.

How did the USA fail to contain communism?

There are 6 main ways the USA was unable to contain communism successfully:

✅ They were unable to contain communism to North Vietnam. Vietnam became, and remained, a united communist country.

✅ Laos and Cambodia also fell to communism.

✅ North Korea remained communist.

✅ Cuba remained communist.

- ☑ Some communist ideas spread to Central America.
- ☑ Stalin was able to maintain huge influence over eastern Europe, and many eastern European countries became communist.

A

Aggression - angry, hostile or violent behaviour displayed without provocation.

Air strike - an attack by aircraft, typically a bombing.

Alliance - a union between groups or countries that benefits each member.

Allies - parties working together for a common objective, such as countries involved in a war. In both world wars, 'Allies' refers to those countries on the side of Great Britain.

Ambassador - someone, often a diplomat, who represents their state, country or organisation in a different setting or place.

Ammunition - collective term given to bullets and shells.

Armistice - an agreement between two or more opposing sides in a war to stop fighting.

Artillery - large guns used in warfare.

Assassinate - to murder someone, usually an important figure, often for religious or political reasons.

Assassination - the act of murdering someone, usually an important person.

Attrition - the act of wearing down an enemy until they collapse through continued attacks.

B

Blockade - a way of blocking or sealing an area to prevent goods, supplies or people from entering or leaving. It often refers to blocking transport routes.

Booby traps - seemingly harmless devices concealing something that will kill, harm or surprise. Especially in warfare, booby traps were often set off by a wire and contained explosives.

Boycott - a way of protesting or bringing about change by refusing to buy something or use services.

Bribe, Bribery, Bribes - to dishonestly persuade someone to do something for you in return for money or other inducements.

Brinkmanship - pushing a disagreement to its limits in the hope the other side backs down, especially pertaining to war.

C

Campaign - a political movement to get something changed; in military terms, it refers to a series of operations to achieve a goal.

Capitalism - the idea of goods and services being exchanged for money, private ownership of property and businesses, and acceptance of a hierarchical society.

Casualties - people who have been injured or killed, such as during a war, accident or catastrophe.

Ceasefire - when the various sides involved in conflict agree to stop fighting.

Censorship - the control of information in the media by a government, whereby information considered obscene or unacceptable is suppressed.

Civil rights - the rights a citizen has to political or social freedoms, such as the right to vote or freedom of speech.

Civilian - a non-military person.

Claim - someone's assertion of their right to something - for example, a claim to the throne.

Communism - the belief, based on the ideas of Karl Marx, that all people should be equal in society without government, money or private property. Everything is owned by by the people, and each person receives according to need.

Communist - a believer in communism.

Conference - a formal meeting to discuss common issues of interest or concern.

Conscription - mandatory enlistment of people into a state service, usually the military.

Containment - meaning to keep something under control or within limits, it often refers to the American idea of stopping the spread of communism.

Corrupt - when someone is willing to act dishonestly for their own personal gain.

Counter-attack - an attack made in response to one by an opponent.

Culture - the ideas, customs, and social behaviour of a particular people or society.

D

Deadlock - a situation where no action can be taken and neither side can make progress against the other; effectively a draw.

Defect - the act of defection; to leave your country or cause for another.

Demilitarised - to remove all military forces from an area and forbid them to be stationed there.

Democracy - a political system where a population votes for its government on a regular basis. The word is Greek for 'the rule of people' or 'people power'.

Democratic - relating to or supporting the principles of democracy.

Deploy - to move military troops or equipment into position or a place so they are ready for action.

Dictator - a ruler with absolute power over a country, often acquired by force.

Dictatorship - a form of government where an individual or small group has total power, ruling without tolerance for other views or opposition.

Disarmament - the reduction or removal of weaponry.

Dispute - a disagreement or argument; often used to describe conflict between different countries.

E

Economic - relating to the economy; also used when justifying something in terms of profitability.

Economy - a country, state or region's position in terms of production and consumption of goods and services, and the supply of money.

Electorate - a group of people who are eligible to vote.

Embassy - historically, a deputation sent by one ruler, state or country to another. More recently, it is also the accepted name for the official residence or offices of an ambassador.

Exile - to be banned from one's original country, usually as a punishment or for political reasons.

F

Fatalities, Fatality - Deaths.

Foreign policy - a government's strategy for dealing with other nations.

Free elections - elections in which voters are free to vote without interference.

Frontier - a line or border between two areas.

G

Guerrilla tactics, Guerrilla warfare - a way of fighting that typically involves hit-and-run style tactics.

Guerrillas - groups of small, independent fighters usually involved in a war against larger, regular military forces.

H

Harvest - the process of gathering and collecting crops.

I

Ideology - a set of ideas and ideals, particularly around political ideas or economic policy, often shared by a group of people.

Import - to bring goods or services into a different country to sell.

Independence, Independent - to be free of control, often meaning by another country, allowing the people of a nation the ability to govern themselves.

Industrial - related to industry, manufacturing and/or production.

Industry - the part of the economy concerned with turning raw materials into into manufactured goods, for example making furniture from wood.

Intercontinental ballistic missile - a guided ballistic missile with a minimum range of 5,500km or 3,400 miles.

L

Legislation - a term for laws when they are considered collectively, for example housing legislation.

Legitimacy, Legitimate - accepted by law or conforming to the rules; can be defended as valid.

Limb - an arm or leg.

M

Mandate - authority to carry out a policy.

Massacre - the deliberate and brutal slaughter of many people.

Mercenary - someone who takes action in order to earn money, rather than out of principle.

Middle class - refers to the socio-economic group which includes people who are educated and have professional jobs, such as teachers or lawyers.

Military force - the use of armed forces.

Militia - an army created from the general population.

Mine - an explosive device usually hidden underground or underwater.

Minister - a senior member of government, usually responsible for a particular area such as education or finance.

Monk - a member of a religious community, often living a simple life of poverty, chastity and work.

Morale - general mood of a group of people.

Morals - a person's set of rules about what they consider right and wrong, used to guide their actions and behaviour.

N

Napalm - a petrol based chemical, used to devastating effect in conflict as it sticks to skin and causes terrible burns.

Nationalisation - the transfer of control or ownership of a sector of industry, such as banking or rail, from the private sector to the state.

Nationalism, Nationalist, Nationalistic - identifying with your own nation and supporting its interests, often to the detriment or exclusion of other nations.

O

Offensive - another way of saying an attack or campaign.

P

POW, Prisoner of war, Prisoners of war - somebody who has been captured and taken prisoner by enemy forces.

Pacification - Making something, or someone, peaceful.

Parliament - a group of politicians who make the laws of their country, usually elected by the population.

Peasant - a poor farmer.

Poll - a vote or survey.

Population - the number of people who live in a specified place.

Poverty - the state of being extremely poor.

Prejudice - prejudgement - when you assume something about someone based on a feature like their religion or skin colour, rather than knowing it as fact.

President - the elected head of state of a republic.

Prevent, Preventative, Preventive - steps taken to stop something from happening.

Propaganda - biased information aimed at persuading people to think a certain way.

Prosecute - to institute or conduct legal proceedings against a person or organisation.

Proxy war - a conflict between two sides acting on behalf of other parties who are not directly involved, but who have usually supplied equipment, arms and/or money.

Psychological - referring to a person's mental or emotional state.

Q

Quarantine - a period of isolation where a person or animal who has or may have a communicable disease is kept away from others.

R

Raid - a quick surprise attack on the enemy.

Rational - when something is based on reason or logic, like science.

Rebels - people who rise in opposition or armed resistance against an established government or leader.

Reconstruction - a period in the USA from 1865-1877 where the southern states were reintegrated through a series of laws.

Reform, Reforming - change, usually in order to improve an institution or practice.

Refugee, Refugees - a person who has been forced to leave where they live due to war, disaster or persecution.

Restoration - to return something to its former owner, place or condition; this includes returning a monarch to the throne or a head of state to government.

Revolution - the forced overthrow of a government or social system by its own people.

Rig, Rigged - politically, to interfere in or fix an election to determine the winner.

S

Sanctions - actions taken against states who break international laws, such as a refusal to trade with them or supply necessary commodities.

Search and destroy, Seek and destroy - a tactic used by the US in Vietnam. Helicopters brought in soldiers who searched out the enemy in a specific area, such as a village, destroyed them, and then left.

Segregation - when people are kept separately from each other - often used in the context of race.

Soviet - an elected workers' council at local, regional or national level in the former Soviet Union. It can also be a reference to the Soviet Union or the USSR.

Sphere of influence - an area or country under the influence of another country.

Stalemate - a situation where no action can be taken and neither side can make progress against the other; effectively a draw.

State, States - an area of land or a territory ruled by one government.

Strategy - a plan of action outlining how a goal will be achieved.

Strike - a refusal by employees to work as a form of protest, usually to bring about change in their working conditions. It puts pressure on their employer, who cannot run the business without workers.

Submission, Submit - a formal surrender and acceptance of a new authority.

Superior - better or higher in rank, status or quality.

T

Tactic - a strategy or method of achieving a goal.

Terrain - a stretch of land and usually used to refer to its physical features, eg mountainous, jungle etc.

Territories, Territory - an area of land under the control of a ruler/ country.

Treaty - a formal agreement, signed and ratified by two or more parties.

V

Veteran, Veterans - an ex-soldier.

Quizzes, amazing exam preparation tools and more at GCSEHistory.com